With Wings as Eagles

WITH WINGS AS EAGLES

HELEN CHAPPELL WHITE

Introduction by Dr. Ralph W. Sockman

RINEHART & Company, Inc.
New York   Toronto

The letters which appear on pages 109, 110, and 111 are reprinted from MEDITATIONS FOR WOMEN, *edited by Jean Beaven Abernethy, copyright MCMXLVII by Stone and Pierce, and reprinted by permission of Abingdon-Cokesbury Press.*

"Grateful acknowledgment is made to the following publishers for permission to quote from their publications:

HARPER & BROTHERS for permission to quote a line from 'Dirge Without Music' from *The Buck in the Snow*, Copyright, 1928, by Edna St. Vincent Millay.

HENRY HOLT & COMPANY for permission to quote a line from 'Fare Well' from Walter de la Mare's *Collected Poems*."

Fourth Printing, April 1959

Published simultaneously in Canada by Clarke, Irwin & Company, Ltd., Toronto

Copyright, 1953, by Helen Chappell White
Printed in the United States
All rights reserved
Library of Congress Catalog Card Number: 52–12109

To those others who also loved the boy who died that September morning over the Baltic Sea, those whom he loved, whom I love—this book is dedicated with deep gratitude.

FOREWORD

Here is a Pilgrim's Progress "through the valley of the shadow of death." With an intensity of feeling almost too deep for words, a mother describes her descent into anguished despair, and then with the restraint of a highly rational mind she traces the steps by which she climbed back to confident faith. Through the years streams of books about death pour across my desk. I cannot recall one that has moved me so deeply.

The author modestly says, "I was not unique; I was not even unusual; and the anatomy of grief as I came to know it follows a familiar pattern. So a common experience may point the way to a common solution."

To be sure, Helen White is not unique in suffering the loss which comes to all who love.

> It singeth low in every heart,
> We hear it each and all,
> A song of those who answer not,
> However we may call.

But she is strikingly unusual in attuning her mind to hear the satisfying answer which eventually came. By spiritualizing the material rather than by seeking to materialize the spiritual, she establishes vital comradeship behind the iron curtain of death.

Because she picks her way through so many experiences common to those who mourn, the author keeps the reader ever in step with her. In these pages we hear all those well-meant words of sympathy which are such weak messengers of comfort to breaking hearts. She weighs them in the balance and shows wherein they are found wanting. I should like to commend this book to my ministerial colleagues if only to restrain them from glib pious expressions and to show them how much grace it takes to help without hurting.

It was the Master of Death who said, "The words that I say unto you, they are spirit and they are life." Something of that living quality throbs through the lines written by this mother whose brave and brilliant son was shot down while flying in the service of his country. The wife of a distinguished college president, she is conversant with the current trends of the best philosophic thought. Her conclusions will stand the severest theological test. But theology here lives and speaks in personal terms. For this reason it fascinates the reader's mind and moves his heart.

The author refers to her writing as an anatomy of grief. Truly she dissects the deepest experiences with superb skill of analysis and interprets them with beautiful clarity. But I should prefer to call this book a Testament of Faith. At least it strengthens my own faith immeasurably. It gives wings to my spirit.

The more I ponder the character of the gay and gallant young Goodrich White and the love of the mother who so understandingly portrays him, the more I share her conviction that "Life cannot be bad; therefore death cannot be bad."

DR. RALPH W. SOCKMAN.

AUTHOR'S PREFACE

This book was written because a boy died in battle.

Yet it is not a war story. The way in which the boy died is even, in a sense, incidental. For this is the story of the effort of one individual to make an intelligent and reasonably satisfactory adjustment to grief and to death. And grief and death do not wait on war, however they may be hastened and dramatized by it.

It must be said that if the story has seemed worth the telling it is not because this effort led to new answers. The problems were age-old and so are the answers. But answers, after all, are new to each man as he first finds them for himself. For me it was brand-new and very strange to discover that a fuller, clearer understanding of death led to a happier, more vital attitude toward life. Led, indeed, to excitingly widened horizons.

Many others have made this discovery before me; probably with less floundering and struggle than I. But I think that perhaps there are even more who have not made it, who never do make it. I think, too, that it is possible that every satisfactory adjustment to a human experience as probable as grief and one as inevitable as death possesses some little general human significance. This, no matter how unimportant the individual may be in himself, or how immemorial the solutions he believes that he has found.

For me the testimony—some of it spoken to me directly, much of it in books—of those who, as searchers, had traveled this road before me, was of immeasurable value in helping me discover my own path. Perhaps this is why I feel that any fresh guideposts to a trail across what so generally appears as a no man's land of trackless darkness might, just might, serve to point a possible way through to someone who has happened to miss the other markers; might, at least, lead him to those markers which pointed the way for me.

With Wings as Eagles

1

In the library of our home stands a big double photograph; two different poses of the same lad. It stands on the piano he owned and loved, and it strikes the visitor's eye immediately upon entering the room.

In one of the poses the boy is smiling. His eyes, above the spreading navigator's wings pinned so precisely on his trim uniform, fairly dance with delighted mirth; he looks

3

young and happy and mischievous. ("Think of something pleasant—of something downright funny!" the photographer had urged. And the boy had looked at his aunt and me, standing interestedly on the side lines, and recalled, with two words, a family joke—one of those sure-fire, always-amusing, perennial jokes most families possess.)

In the other pose he holds himself stiffly erect, consciously grim and martial, very much aware of the dignity of being an Air Corps officer.

It was early in nineteen forty-seven and our guest was a kindly lady from another state. She was visiting this college community because her son was a student here, and now she paused before the pictures to smile at them and say pleasant things about them.

"I imagine," she observed with a twinkle, "that I know which one *he* prefers."

"Oh, the serious one, of course," I agreed, smiling back at her.

"Is he blond?" she asked. "He looks blond—but of course it's hard to tell in a black and white photograph."

"Quite blond. Real Scandinavian type. His eyes were deep blue from babyhood and they never changed or faded. His skin was very fair and his hair almost flaxen——"

I stopped. I'd used the past tense unconsciously and now I saw her face understandably change and stiffen under the shock of it. So I said quickly,

"Please don't mind—I'm so glad you asked about him.

4

I'm like most mothers—it's fun to talk about my children. We had two sons—both flyers. This is the one that didn't come back."

She had turned a little white.

"Oh, how terrible!" she faltered. "Oh, I'm so sorry—oh, please do forgive me—I wouldn't have for the world . . . "

"But there's no reason to feel like that," I insisted gently. "I meant it when I said I like to talk about him. After all, we don't keep his picture here to distress our friends; we keep it because he's part of the home and because we like for them to see him here and know about him."

She was inconsolable, still convinced that she had made a painful blunder.

"I know you must be proud," she stammered unhappily. "I meant—reminding you, you know—I wouldn't have, not for anything . . ." She broke off in incoherent sympathy. "I don't see how anybody *stands* a thing like that—I know I *couldn't*."

I did not say that she need not be troubled about having "reminded" me of something which was part of the very fabric of myself. Nor did I reply that one had no choice about "standing" things once they had happened. Actually, these were facts she knew as well as I. And by what she had said, she had meant merely that she was very sorry for me, distressed to have bared a wound. I knew this because the echo of my own voice came back to me (as it had often done in these last two years) saying exactly the same things to other people "in trouble"—as I had put it—in the past.

But some answer I must make her. And because there was a great urge in me not to be, at any time when a really favorable chance came, altogether silent as to the faith I held, I said:

"It's hard to take, awfully hard, harder than anyone who hasn't had to take it can know. But there are lots of things that help. Not at first—but finally. The biggest of them is that one does find out, in time, that the loss isn't complete." Here she looked so blank that I added, "I mean, he isn't entirely gone. We still have him—in a different sort of way."

"Oh!" she breathed pityingly. "Oh! How brave you are! How wonderful of you! It's grand to feel that way—I mean, it's certainly a fine Christian attitude—if you can manage to take it, I mean . . ."

But now she was embarrassed, and I was too. She looked at me anxiously, clearly fearful that her last sentence might have seemed to cast a doubt on the authenticity of what I believed, and not wanting to take away from me anything whatsoever that brought me comfort. As for me, I felt as if I had probably sounded smug and pious, and I particularly dislike sounding either one; it's a sort of self-consciousness, on my part, I suppose.

"My dear old grandmother," she offered after a moment, courageous in spite of embarrassment, "always told me that *she* believed that the spirits of our departed loved ones were hovering constantly near us."

Quite sincerely I appreciated the genuine eagerness of her kind intent. It was, moreover, unreasonable of me to feel even more embarrassed than I had before, because actually that is, in essence, just what I myself believe. But it was no use; it didn't *sound* to me like my belief. It sounded like something quite different and something I didn't find attractive. Expressions like "spirits" and "departed loved ones" and "hovering near" have a curiously paralyzing sort of mental effect on me; I hardly know why, though I might make a guess. I realized that it might well be that the time-worn phrases had represented a vivid reality to the lady's grandmother. But not for me. For me they dimmed reality.

Especially that word "spirit." Used in reference to the physically dead, it carries for me a connotation that is ghostly and nebulous. This meaning may not be inherent in the word itself, but it is there for me, and I do not think that I am unusual in having attached this aura to it; I think most people feel the same way, consciously or unconsciously. . . . A "spirit" is something at the best cloudy and unreal, at the worst a bit weird and awesome.

I could not think of the boy whose face smiled at us from the piano like that. Easier, easier for me, to imagine the bright flame of his life as quite extinguished than to see it, in fancy, flickering with this pallid light, see him "hovering near," a pallid wraith.

So I sighed, a very brief, inaudible sigh, and then smiled brightly at my kind acquaintance.

7

"Yes," I said politely. "I'm sure it was a comfort to her. Oh, by the way—on the desk—behind you, on the other side of the room—there's a picture of our other son, another double photograph in uniform. He's in the East now—doing graduate work. I'm going to visit him soon."

Her relief was instant and spontaneous; she flashed me a look of pure, unconscious gratitude. She said eagerly and delightedly that she was *so* glad I was going to have a visit with him, and she turned quickly to look at his picture, and to comment (Such a kindhearted person! Her voice was unsteady as she did so) on his smile and his curly hair and to assure me that he "looked like a darling." We could talk about *him,* and it was a great comfort to her to bring his warm, living, young presence into the room with us.

She was what is called "a good church woman" and she was genuinely devout. Her theological beliefs, I am sure, were orthodox; which means that she would have stoutly maintained that "immortality" was a solid fact. Not for a moment would she have admitted that the dead had utterly ceased to be.

And yet it was perfectly clear that also not for a moment did her heart agree with her theology. Her heart felt that the boy whose picture smiled at us from the piano was completely dead and gone; and even while that tender heart shuddered with pity, it longed to turn away from the contemplation of the tragedy.

I did not wonder at this. I had once felt the same way. Be-

8

sides I knew how much secret fear was mingled with that shrinking. But I was sorry. I would have liked to chat with her, cheerfully and normally, about that boy—as we had chatted about her children, as we could chat about my other son.

Not very long ago a visiting preacher shook my hand at a party and inquired for our sons, whom, he said, he had not seen for many years. Because I knew that the news about Goodrich would naturally cast a shadow on a pleasant social occasion, I made an effort to dodge by speaking only of the younger boy.

"Well, Chap is in the East studying now——" I began, but he interrupted me.

"Splendid, splendid! But it was Goodrich I knew best. Where is he now?"

I tried to keep him from feeling the agonized embarrassment at having asked which I'd encountered before. I told him that I was so glad that he had asked, that it always pleased me when people did. And I gave him the story as simply and matter-of-factly as I could.

I was prepared, of course, for the shocked dismay which overspread his face; any other reaction would have seemed a bit inhuman. But I was not quite prepared for him to stammer a broken "Sorry—so very sorry—didn't know—" and, adding something incoherent about seeing a man before he left, literally and precipitately flee. There was just an instant, before his eyes swerved from mine, that I had the fancy that I saw in them something of pleading, as if silently, unaware that he did so, he begged me to try to understand.

And I think I did understand. I understood his real, kindly, human distress. I understood his sensitive apprehension lest he had unwittingly, with clumsy hand, dealt a stab. And I understood the deep horror of death which lay behind that involuntary flight.

Being a thoroughly good man and a conscientious shepherd, he would probably reproach himself later, wondering why he had behaved that way and laying it, no doubt, to shock. In a sense he would be right in so doing. Part of his job was to "comfort the bereaved," and visits of "consolation" and the conducting of funeral services could have been nothing unusual in his life. If he had had time to marshal his attitudes and his phrases, they would have been quite different. He did not have time, and so he reacted as he felt, and he felt like escaping.

If I looked after him a bit sadly, it was not, of course, that I would have wished or expected him to offer to pray with me at a social occasion. No, it was only that I could not help remembering that a few years ago I had watched such dedicated ones as he with the almost feverish hope that they might be able to share with me some measure of the sunny, confident faith I assumed was theirs. I assumed it because I knew that their lives and all their efforts were publicly committed to the propagation of a religion which is rooted and grounded in the belief that nobody really dies, which actually would cease to have any meaning or existence if this foundation were taken away. These men were, in a sense, ambassadors from another country. Surely then, my unformulated hope ran, surely there might be—even in a chance, passing contact—some quick word or look, some atmosphere of reassurance and of certain faith, to warm and hearten and encourage.

Occasionally I had found it. And always, when it came, it had brought an indescribable lift of the heart to me; brought indeed, in those early, difficult days, a relief for a while, at least, that was almost like the relief from severe physical pain—that same lightheaded sense of intolerable pressure easing. If I was not able at that time to keep it, still I think it was far truer than I knew that I did not wholly lose it, and that each time some permanent residue was left.

But usually I had looked vainly for evidence that death was any less fearful or that other country any more real to these professionally spiritual visions than to my own secular one. Perhaps I misinterpreted, perhaps I was wrong. Nevertheless it seemed to me to be a fact—and a fact which always made my own darkness appear deeper and blacker.

Even the people who've staked their lives on it can't manage really to believe it, I'd think desolately. Because if they did, death would have to seem at least a little bit less terrible and final a catastrophe to *them*—and it doesn't, it doesn't! No matter what they honestly suppose they believe, it's clear that to them, just as to the rest of us, death looks like the end of everything.

So today, remembering this, it seemed sad to me that this good man who said so sincerely every Sunday, "I believe in the life everlasting," actually, though probably unconsciously, viewed the entrance to that life with such deep fear and hatred. It seemed sad, too, that most other people felt the same way.

For if an event which is natural, inevitable, imminent and universal is also the most crushing disaster which can possibly befall any human being, then mankind is in a sorry plight. A permanently sorry plight from which there is no conceivable escape no matter how much better, stronger and wiser he may become as the ages pass.

"I wish I understood about you!" a young friend of mine in another city said to me about two years ago.

"Understood what about me?" I asked, puzzled.

We were sitting on her porch and her gaze—faintly troubled, I thought—went to where her children played in the yard.

"I probably can't explain—I shouldn't have spoken. But —well, I saw you after the terrible news about Goodrich. You looked—awful." She seemed to shiver a little. "I watched you at a party one night. I had the oddest feeling. It was as if somebody in the midst of a major operation without an anesthetic was trying to carry on a pleasant social conversation, you were going through all the motions but I knew that the only thing that was very real to you was your own pain. And I understood—I understood in a kind of dreadful way. But now I don't."

12

I waited, still puzzled.

"It's only," she said evasively, "that I have two boys of my own, you know. You seem perfectly all right now, but that's not what I mean. People do get over things, I know, though how a mother could . . ."

I had used that phrase "get over it" often myself in the past. I was not quite sure today what I had meant by it—nor what she meant by it. Perhaps we meant "forget." I had not forgotten my son. But I did not say so now. I still waited, wanting to find out just what was in her mind.

"It's not that you seem all right, it's that you seem almost *better* than you did before!" she burst out accusingly. (Not that she meant to sound accusing nor knew she did.) "I could understand resignation and a certain serenity. I guess I could, anyway. Though a boy like that—it seems like if his mother cried all her life, it wouldn't be too much. But anyway—what I'm trying to say—well, after you seemed to stop grieving for him, it was as if you got a new vitality—I mean, more than you'd had! And that's what I simply don't get! That you could go on cheerfully enough after enough time had passed, that's just being decently brave and unselfish, I can see. Everybody should try to do that, of course. But to be actually gay again, to seem to enjoy life, to be as much—no, more—alive than you were before—after he had to die so tragically and so young . . ."

She came to a headlong pause, and sent me a suddenly stricken look.

13

"Oh forgive me!" she wailed. "It's just that I don't say it right. I'm so glad you're all right, so happy about it, really. It's just my horrid way of trying to figure everything out —and it sounds as if I'm criticizing you. I'm not, please believe me I'm not!"

But she was. To her, try as she might not to feel it, what she had been describing seemed a strange and even cruel disloyalty.

One understands—fully—a feeling one has once fully experienced. I wanted very much to explain to her, but where could I start?

I said, after a moment, "If it's true that I have some small extra quality as a human being that I didn't have before, I'm glad. Because that's the sort of memorial I want to raise to him."

There was an instant's blank silence. Then she answered flatly, "Oh! Yes—I see."

But she didn't see. Her eyes were empty.

It was then that I suddenly wanted to try to tell the whole story.

2

One rather odd quirk of human nature is that as our personalities change and develop we almost completely forget the feel of our own outgrown attitudes and opinions. We can, often reluctantly, recall that we certainly did feel and act in a particular manner; but why we felt like that or how on earth we could have acted so, baffles us as much as if, or perhaps

15

even more than if, we were considering the case of another individual.

I, for instance, can find no sort of reasonable explanation for the fact that an averagely intelligent human being (I cling to the notion that I am that) reached the age of forty without once having consciously faced death as a personal, emotional reality. Yet I know that this is what I did. Up to that time there had been no break in my intimate family circle; and apparently I had by then, through some curious feat of mental legerdemain I cannot now pretend to understand, achieved the peculiar emotional conviction that death was a business so extremely remote from me and everyone for whom I cared deeply, as to be— for all practical purposes—no personal concern of mine.

I did not know that I had this conviction. I did not even know that I passionately feared and hated death. If one had told me I did, I would almost certainly have replied incredulously:

"How can I be afraid of it when I hardly ever think about it?"

That this question was in itself a sort of admission of fear; that it was, to say the least, strange that I had been able to live in the world for forty years meeting death—as does everyone—at every turn and constantly seeing it strike all about me, and *not* "think about it"—these were considerations I was not, at that time, prepared to entertain.

And I must repeat that this "conviction" of which I

speak was unconscious and emotional. Consciously and intellectually I was, of course, quite clear on the point; I knew that everything that lives must die. I simply chose, in certain deeply felt personal areas, not to apply what I knew. I was not unique in this wish and effort. Eluding and ignoring unpleasant facts, turning one's back on what one wishes heartily not to see, are not inventions of mine alone, but habits of a large share of the human race. So my puzzlement does not arise from the fact that I wanted to do it, but that I was able to do it so thoroughly.

That I did do it thoroughly, however, there is no doubt. So successfully that though I was deeply distressed when death struck at my friends, and shaken by agonized sympathy at certain stories I read in the newspapers, it all—in my mind—remained something quite outside of any conceivable experience of mine. In effect I had built a fortress, I had drawn a magic circle; and within that fortress and that circle contrived (I wonder how!) to feel absurdly, idiotically safe.

The first two real breaches in my defense were painful but did not leave me unable to repair and rebuild. For those first two times that death laid his finger on me, it was with a gentle touch. My mother died in her early seventies, my father three years later when he was just past eighty.

I not only loved my parents dearly but I admired them tremendously. I thought that they were delightful and highly superior human beings and I was intensely proud of them. I seemed to grow oddly older after they were gone (I myself was the "older generation" now and there was no longer anyone to whom I was "Child") and there was a heavy sense of change and loss which persisted for long. I knew deeply that something fine and valuable had ended and that the quality of our family life was, and would continue to be, the poorer for that ending.

Nevertheless, it is still true that the touch was gentle. Passionately and determinedly unadjusted as I was to death, no normal adult can be wholly unadjusted to the idea that his parents will die before he does. It is in the expected course of things, it is the natural procedure, something he has always known, and simply takes for granted without formulating. From the time he was quite small he has heard them make remarks like, "We want to get our house paid for and have something to leave you children," and "After we're gone . . ." However painful the idea, it cannot possibly be unfamiliar, and some degree of subconscious adaptation to it normally does take place. This is so true that those grown-up sons and daughters who, as we say, "go to pieces" over the death of an aged mother or father are usually assumed to have lacked the other ordinary close relationships of maturity.

So unless our parents die long before we might reasonably expect, or unless they die violently, there is no great, unexpected shock in their going, however profound the sadness, however irrevocable the loss. Death in old age is felt, almost instinctively, to be somehow fitting; and it may be easier for love to bear than the piteous sight of mental or physical disintegration which must sometimes be faced.

In my case, my parents' lives had been peculiarly happy and fortunate, almost signally lacking in any major troubles or griefs or defeats, and when they left us, their going was peaceful and painless. My mother was smiling radiantly as she drifted off into the coma that preceded her death. What she saw behind her closed lids I cannot know, but she was murmuring over and over, "Beautiful! Oh, how beautiful! So—so—beautiful!"

My father was actually ill only one day. Early one morning, getting up to pull down his shade, he slipped and fell and broke his hip. That night at six o'clock his heart stopped suddenly. For most of that last day he was unconscious or semiconscious. But there was an interval, after he had been given morphine to ease the pain, when he was comfortable and mentally clear. He wanted to talk; he had some directions to give me; and finally, quite matter-of-factly, even with a certain grave contentment, he told me that he was sure this was the end.

He had been the darling of the family in the three years since my mother's going; an utterly gentle, serene, old man whose presence cast a kind of mellow benignity wherever he went. In his prime he had been a man of impatient temper, but the years, which sometimes bring fretfulness and restlessness, had brought to him an ever-growing peace and stability. Watching him, I had learned that if one is a certain sort of person, the time comes when one no longer needs to *do* in order to be useful and loved; it is enough to be. Just by being what he was, my father changed the atmosphere of any home in which he lived, even of any room he entered.

"Only to see him come into church every Sunday with his grandsons made the whole week better for me," said a businessman who scarcely knew him personally, after his death.

So that day, seeing something sweet and lovely slipping from my life for the second time, I began to sob.

"Don't!" he begged distressed. "Please don't."

I tried to stop and couldn't.

"Listen, darling," he said. "I'll tell you a secret. I haven't wanted to say it before, but I'm getting just a little bit impatient to go."

"No!" I cried in involuntary reproach. "No!"

"But why not?" he asked. "You mustn't spoil it for me by grieving—how can I go happily if you're like this? And why should you grieve, anyway? We're Christians, aren't we?"

He was, oh *he* was! It didn't seem the moment to tell him how uncertain I felt about my own status.

I stammered, "It doesn't seem to help—somehow."

"It will, though," he promised confidently. "It has to, you know." Then quite suddenly he broke into a smile, genuine, amused, even with a touch of gentle mischief.

"And anyway," he finished, "we're rational people, aren't we? You didn't expect me to live forever, did you?"

My understanding of a faith like his was more imperfect than I realized; and even dimmer was my comprehension of that fine sense of values, that splendid sanity and poise that could take death calmly in its stride as a natural, wholesome development of life. Yet even so, I felt in that instant such a triumphant thrill of surging pride in him that something deeper than my grief, wiser than my fear, knew clearly that what I was watching was not tragedy. It was as if, for one flash, I had looked squarely into the face of my enemy and had seen wonderingly—before the fleeting insight passed and was forgotten and denied— that it was not hideous and fearsome, after all, that it even held a strange beauty.

We buried my father beside my mother in the city where their home had been. After the funeral we, his four children, sat about rather drearily in a hotel room before separating to return to our own different homes. Our husbands, wives, and the grandchildren had tactfully left us alone for these few moments, supposing there might be family matters about which we wished to confer; but we seemed to have little to say just now.

There was the tall brother from Texas who looked so much like his father, the eldest; he sat by the window, his long fingers restlessly tapping the sill. There was the sister who, luckily for me, lived only a few doors from me in

Atlanta; she had always been "the pretty one" and she was pretty now as she sat very quietly wiping away tears. And there was Edwin, the youngest of us, who was perched beside me on the bed.

There were only fourteen months between me and this brother, who had always seemed more like my twin. I looked at him now, big and blond and very blue-eyed, and wondered what unknown forebear had looked like that. One of them, certainly; for he and my elder son were strikingly, even remarkably, like each other and not like anyone else in the family connection. He caught my eye and grinned suddenly.

"I've just had one very cheering thought," said he. "I've been looking at all of you and reflecting that no matter how old I grow, each of you is always going to be still older."

It did exactly what he meant it to do; we laughed, and suddenly the atmosphere in the room grew warmer, more natural. Then he pulled from his pocket the heavy gold watch which the parishioners of one of my father's first churches had given him many years ago— "From a grateful congregation," the inscription read.

"Dad left this to me," he said, "because it has his name on it and mine is the same. But it seems he promised it to your oldest hopeful next, Helen . . ."

He laughed and we looked at him inquiringly.

"The kid reminded me of it just now," he explained. "He was right cute. I gathered he thought it wouldn't be

22

long. I suppose with nothing between him and it but a decrepit old uncle past forty, he feels it's as good as his right now."

The small incident has stayed in the memories of us all; partly because the manner of its telling was so typical of Edwin, and partly because it was indeed not long before "the kid" got the watch—but neither did he himself keep it for long.

There is no way to put into words the warmth of personality. Edwin had to a remarkable degree the gift of sympathy and of friendliness. He was an utterly approachable human being, and everybody he touched even in fleeting and trivial ways seemed to feel and respond to this quality. Perhaps the closest one can come to expressing it is to say that there seemed to be no barriers at all between him and the rest of humanity.

I used to think, with affectionate amusement, that he could not so much as stop for gas on the highway without receiving a lot of confidences. He was continually involved in other people's affairs for the simple reason that they were always bringing them to him and it never occurred to him to extricate himself. He seemed always to be hunting a job or an apartment or something-or-other for somebody, and I've been in his home when a despondent friend waked him at two o'clock in the morning to sob out over the telephone that his wife had left him.

That was Edwin. He was happy in the way people who think little about themselves and much about others are happy, and he loved living. I think that even the tough spots interested him, and I cannot imagine his ever having been bored. He loved it all. And he died in an hour.

The night before his death he had been watering his roses and playing badminton. That afternoon he was to go on a trip to New York. The tickets were in his billfold. It was Sunday morning, a bright September day. His French wife was happily getting their breakfast in the gay little red kitchen of which they were so proud, when suddenly he called and told her he was afraid he must be sick. . . .

Half an hour later our telephone rang three hundred miles away. I answered it a bit drowsily; I was just out of bed. Then I went rigid. A strange voice was saying stranger words. Somebody seemed to be telling me that he was a doctor and that my brother had just had a heart attack.

"A—*what?*"

The voice repeated, "A heart attack."

"*Edwin?*" I said incredulously. "But it isn't serious——"

The voice contradicted flatly, "It's very serious. I'm sorry. His wife asked me to telephone you. It's doubtful if he pulls through."

I hung the receiver up abruptly. It was a curious reaction which I was to duplicate a few years later. As if I felt that by severing the connection, I might somehow deny the message.

I walked back into my room, sat down on the edge of my

bed, and stared stupidly before me in an amazement so vast that for the moment it literally swallowed up every other sensation. My husband was here now, asking quickly and anxiously, "What was it?"

"It was a doctor. In Nashville. He was saying—he seemed to be saying . . ."

Realization of exactly what it was the doctor had been saying swept me then; belatedly, with shattering force. I came frantically to my feet.

"Call back!" I cried. "He was saying—why, he was saying that Edwin is dying and that can't possibly be true!" (Edwin was inside my magic circle—Edwin couldn't die.) "Oh call back, please—quick!"

It took some moments to get the connection again; I waited, trembling, murmuring at intervals, "He couldn't have got as sick as this so quickly. Some doctors are alarmists. . . . We saw him just last week. . . . He was perfectly well then. . . . He can't be that sick . . ."

But when my husband finally did get the doctor again, Edwin was dead.

And somewhere on the road between Atlanta and Nashville on that dreadfully beautiful, blue-and-gold September day, I remember thinking:

"Now I know that anybody can die."

3

A few years earlier my husband's fine young brother-in-law had died after an illness of more than five years. It had hurt us all deeply, for ourselves and for his incredibly gallant wife. But Doug had been sick for so long and his sickness had been from the first so hopeless that when the end came we had tried to tell ourselves—in that rather vague and unsatisfying phrase people use—that he was "better off."

26

Edwin's case was different. He had apparently died in the glow of radiant health. I could not possibly imagine that he was "better off." Nor could I attain even the smallest measure of that gentle, mellow quality—that sense of sweetness and fittingness—which had characterized my grief for my parents. This was just raw, rebellious, bewildered pain.

Bewildered most of all, perhaps. My head knew but my heart could not understand how it could be Edwin who was dead. I repeatedly found myself saying stupidly to myself, "There must be some mistake—he isn't the sort of person who dies." Yet he *was* dead, and there seemed to be no way to integrate that awkward, hurting fact into my life. The trouble was that if I could not integrate it, neither could I dispose of it. It remained an odd-shaped, jagged piece in my personal pattern of things, one which fitted nowhere, one whose sharp points must continue to stab.

"Anybody can die." There was a corollary to that: "Everybody will die." It was precisely this corollary which I can see, looking back, that I was still trying desperately not to face. For once you did face it, squarely and plainly, once you truly learned it (oh, not with your mind which had always known it, but with your heart and blood and breath and very bones!), then how did you manage afterwards to go on living with any sort of hope or courage? How *could* you? How could anybody? What would be the use of even trying? All of life would then have become no more than a *danse macabre,* or truer still a sort of tightrope which one walked, a tightrope stretched across a terrifyingly black, an utterly mysterious and fearful canyon. And since there was no secure other side which one could hope to reach, since the canyon stretched on into forever, all one's painful, precarious balancing was useless, after all. No matter how carefully one picked one's way, that inevitable next step which would some-day plunge one into the canyon below was not far off. The dark depths waited for everybody, oneself and all one loved. Oh, I cried passionately, Whatever made us, Whatever put us here, It had no right to make the conditions under which we must exist so intolerable!

When a human being finds himself confronted with conditions that seem to him intolerable, he may react in a number of ways. He may crumple helplessly; he may meet them with grim, if hopeless, courage; he may fight and try to master them; he may search for an intelligent way out of them; he may resign himself to them; or he may try to escape from them. Eventually I chose (not, of course, either deliberately or consciously) the last expedient. It was, indeed, the same one I had always chosen. The question was whether this time I could achieve it.

Was there any way to salvage at least a modicum of the old sense of safety? How if one drew the magic circle again but much, oh much, smaller this time? Could death be placated by some concessions? Could one manage to face just a little bit of the inevitable but not the horrifying whole of it?

I think I must have asked questions like this somewhere far, far down in my subconscious. They sound fantastic, but human nature becomes fantastic when it dodges and twists and turns in the effort not to see the thing which it knows is there, the thing it cannot actually avoid seeing. Denying reality involves quite a lot of fantasy. Yes—I must have asked the questions, and I must have answered them; because I did, to a degree and in time, redraw my magic circle.

Perhaps it is true that I no longer dared place within its shelter any of my contemporaries—except my husband, simply because it was impossible to leave *him* out. Perhaps I had conceded that elders and contemporaries, even when very dear to me, must die. Certainly the circle's dimensions were shrunken. But it included, besides my husband (and perhaps by implication myself), the few young people—my sons and some others—whom I loved. And gradually that curious emotional conviction that at least "nothing would happen" (the oddly ambiguous phrase one uses!) to *them* lulled one area of my mind to sleep again.

This splendid reconstruction of a house built on sand was completed just in time. December seventh, 1941, was barely around the corner, and both my sons were to enter the Air Corps as combat flyers. By the time that happened I was able to tell myself that "everything would be all right," that I was not in the least afraid; and, indeed, consciously I was not.

Yet curiously enough, a few years later, in a black hour, I was to cry out something wild and strange without realizing what it meant; something which might have shown me that in one of those hidden levels of my mind I had known quite clearly all the time exactly at what date I actually stopped living in that Never-Never Land of mine. "It mightn't have happened if Edwin hadn't died!" I cried. "That's when everything went wrong, that's when everything sad and bad and cruel began!"

The day came, of course, when my enemy overtook me again. The day came when Death was there beyond conciliating or ignoring any longer, never again by any sort of hocus-pocus to be relegated to my unconscious, not even a dark figure that lurked half-seen in the shadows now, but one that walked boldly beside me in the open light.

That day was December twenty-ninth, 1944. But first, as its forerunner and herald, there came September twenty-sixth of that same year.

I was at my typewriter that morning. Yesterday we'd had a letter from Goodrich, who was flying and fighting in Europe now, based in England. It had been a long letter, begun on the tenth and finished on the eleventh. He'd interrupted it to bicycle to the little English village near by with his pal—"Bill found a piano we could use and we played till 'way after midnight." He'd just received a decoration and was being rather carefully casual about that. "In the Air Corps they give 'em to you for staying alive!" He and Bill thought maybe they'd buy a cocker puppy together; it cost fifteen pounds and they could bring it home with them, one or the other of them, when they came—what did I think of that?

I'd lunched with friends yesterday and had taken the letter with me and read parts of it aloud, proudly, to them. Now I was cheerfully engaged in copying it to send to Chap, who was momently expecting his own orders to fly overseas.

When I had finished, I would copy Chap's latest for Goodrich. That was the one in which he had written that he was feeling pretty blue. "A bomber exploded here yesterday, just after it took off. All the poor fellows in it were lost. I knew some of them and liked them. Makes you feel awful."

Just now I had reached the sentences in Goodrich's letter that began, "The last mission was the toughest we've had. The flak was unusually heavy—tore a big hole one foot from where I sit—and we lost the target and had to circle back," when some slight noise made me stop and look up. My husband was standing in the doorway. Just standing there.

It was only ten thirty; he did not usually come home till at least twelve thirty. Besides, like most husbands he generally called "Hi!" almost the moment he opened the door. He had not called today. He stood looking at me silently.

Did something stir deep down inside me then? I've often wondered. It seems so incredible that it should not have. But I can only say in complete honesty that if it did, I was not aware of it. So thoroughly had I anesthetized a certain portion of my consciousness that I was merely slightly surprised; and I cannot recall one twinge of alarm.

"Hello!" I said amiably. "Home early, aren't you?"

He came across the room then; he put his arm around me before he spoke. His voice was strange. He said just two words, "It's come." And I answered with just two, frowning in puzzlement, "What's come?"

Then I saw that he held in his hand the yellow slip of paper that means a telegram. But even then I did not say, "The boys—?" No, I did not even *think* "The boys!"

His throat moved but he did not speak. Instead he unfolded the slip and spread it before me. . . . The Secretary of War deeply regretted to inform us that our son, Lieutenant Goodrich C. White, Jr., was missing in action as of September twelfth after a mission over Czecho-Slovakia; we would be kept informed of any further developments.

"No," I said. "No! No! No!"

Then, after a little, through chattering teeth, "We must telephone Chap but we mustn't frighten him. Of course Goodrich is a prisoner and we'll hear before too long— we must tell Chap we're sure of that."

In October we went to Washington. Chap was now on his way overseas. I talked at length to a kindly major in Casualties.

"Of course," I explained, swallowing a little, "we do feel practically certain Goodrich is in a German prison camp. Such a large per cent of the missing airmen do turn up like that. But—but—it would help if we could get just a little more information. So I wondered—if maybe . . ."

The major said he'd see. He left me for a while and came back with a sheet in his hand. He was sorry he couldn't do better; there really was not much. He looked down at the sheet.

"The ship radioed back to the base in England at about eleven thirty on the morning of the twelfth that she had been injured over Berlin and could not keep up with the formation. She was therefore, the message said, considering turning back to England. At that time none of the crew were injured. However, the bomber did not return, as you know, and there has been no further news of her."

That was all he told me. There was something else he might have told me; for two families represented on that bomber had already received news—the pilot's wife and the copilot's mother had heard. But this he did not mention and indeed I suppose he could not have done so; regulations would not have permitted. Nor would it have helped, actually.

Scanty as the news was, it seemed to me intensely heartening. I wept a little, there in the Casualties office

33

which must have seen so many tears, and then apologized, sending the major a tremulously radiant little smile.

"Maybe I was a bit more worried than I knew," I admitted. "And now—well, this seems to make it certain they're all safe—just that they had to land and were taken prisoner—and it's—maybe it's a bigger relief than I realized."

"Yes—well . . ." said the major.

I wiped my eyes and asked hopefully, "How soon do you suppose we can expect to hear from him?"

"I have no idea." He did not look happy. He said abruptly, "You know your picture could be—ah—a little too rosy. There are many other things that might have happened. Things different from what you have described. Less fortunate."

I answered quickly, "Oh, of course I do realize that."

But I lied. I did not realize it and I had no intention of realizing it. I merely told myself that it was the major's duty to warn me, but that the warning had no significance.

We came back home. The days crept slowly by. Three other boys in our neighborhood who had also been reported missing the last week in September were now reported prisoners of war. I telephoned to congratulate their mothers and the mothers said, "Your turn next," and I replied brightly that I was sure it wouldn't be long. Chap wrote often from England, and we wrote almost every day to him, and each morning when we got up we said, "Maybe—today . . ." and each night when we went to bed we said, "Well—perhaps, tomorrow . . ."

Once a week I wrote to Goodrich and carefully filed the letter away. "I want to keep a little chronicle of these days for you to read when you come home," I had written in the first one. "For one thing I might forget to tell you all about the letters and the wires and the telephone calls and the flowers. You might never really know just how important you are."

Writing it, I'd smiled to myself, knowing what he'd answer to that. "Huh! Because I'm missing. Just wait till I turn up and you'll see how little importance I have!" And I'd say, with a happy lump in my throat, "You're plenty important *enough*." Which last belonged in what *The New Yorker* would call the Department of Understatement.

Early in November our French sister received word that her younger sister, Germaine, had been killed just before D-Day by an American bomb. I had met Germaine, plump and pretty and gay, and I grieved with Jeannot. I was grateful that neither of her American nephews had ever had to bomb France; they loved France and they loved their French aunt. But even so Chap, in combat now and carrying his own heavy load of suspense, seemed to feel a curious sense of guilt about it which touched us all. "I am heartbroken for you, Petite," he wrote, "and all the boys in my crew want to send their sympathy, too. Forgive us—me—them—all of us over here who are doing our clumsy best."

"Oh, the poor kid—why would he think I'd feel like that?" Jeannot said with weary sadness. "I'm not bitter about anything but war. Anyway, who wanted to kill Germaine—my sweet fat little Germaine? Nobody, of course."

I looked at her worn face and felt again that passionate resentment against the fact of death which I'd felt when Douglas died, when Edwin died.

It was December now. Chap wrote, "I can't seem to get interested in the war or missions or anything much except whether there'll be news of *him*. I think about him all the time with an intensity that makes everything else seem a little dim and hazy."

I was losing flesh, in spite of my persistent hopefulness. My husband went about his exacting job with his usual steadiness, but he looked older. I set my teeth and told myself over and over that all this would end someday. It was a bad stretch, a terribly bad stretch that had to be lived through. It was a nightmare, but the very essential quality of nightmares was that they didn't last, that they weren't real. The relieved waking to the lovely, everyday, beautifully ordinary world one knew so well—that was what was real. That was what would happen. The anxiety about the boy who was fighting, the suspense about the boy who was missing, would all be past, and I'd remember it only as one recalls an especially bad dream, saying with a shiver, "Thank God it's over!"

After all, I reminded myself, I had lived through suspense before. Everybody had. Serious illnesses of one's family, hours when one waited at a hospital, times when the children got hurt or lost—these were just the ordinary events of a lifetime which everyone sooner or later (and usually both sooner and later) must experience. Thinking of it like this, I realized that all the symptoms were familiar: the nagging nausea, the shivery stomach, the cold hands, the strange aspect the world took on—a sort of different color and texture—so that even well-known scenes looked oddly unnatural . . . yes, I recognized them all. And this time, I kept assuring myself, this time was actually not different in quality from those other times. It was the quantity of the experience only that had changed. Three months was quite a long time—to live in acute suspense.

Long, but not unbearably long. I remembered Jeannot's story of her soldier brother; she had interrupted one of his Army tales to ask, "But Constant, how could you possibly walk that far with a pack weighing that much on your back?" And he had answered meditatively, "Well, I don't know how myself, except that there never seemed to be any reason why I shouldn't put one foot before another just one more time."

That was what I had to do now; keep on putting one foot

before another just one more time—and suddenly one day the bad stretch would be behind me.

"It was pretty tough," I'd say, someday, to the boy who was missing in action now, "but of course I always felt sure that you'd come back and that Chap would get through safely—somehow I just *knew*." And he'd answer, "I told myself you'd feel like that."

It turned bitterly cold as December advanced. The newspapers reported that there was almost no coal in Germany and less food and that the suffering from cold and hunger was severe.

Ordinarily I would have read that statement with a pang of painful pity. But now my imagination was concentrated so intensely on one figure which I pictured as in Germany, that there was room in my mind for only one overwhelming thought: If they haven't got food or fuel for themselves, dear God, what's happening to their prisoners?

Later I read that Red Cross packages were no longer able to reach prisoners through Switzerland because the railroads had been so drastically bombed, and that an American prisoner in Germany was lucky to get one sliver of black bread and a bowl of watery cabbage soup per day. It was after this that I suddenly pushed my plate away from me one night at dinner, choking.

"It's no use—I can't eat. When I think that maybe all *he* has had today is black bread and cabbage soup——"

In the long, pitying look my husband sent me then, there was a tinge of wonder.

"I wish," he said slowly, "I wish to God I knew that he'd been eating black bread and cabbage soup today!"

It was nearly Christmas. It was nearly December twenty-ninth.

4

At Christmas we went to New Orleans. There were no lights wreathing our door that year, no candles burning gold and red and blue in our windows, no glitter of a Christmas tree.

"We'll make up for it next year," I said confidently.

Goodrich had been missing for more than three months and the darkness that had swallowed him was still unpierced by any gleam of light. My husband said nothing.

In New Orleans for three days we wandered around the French Quarter and ate in the famous restaurants. But we never stayed away from the hotel for more than an hour or two at a time because of the message that might, at any moment, be relayed from home.

One day we strolled through an old cemetery and at one grave I lingered for so long that my husband, a little distance away, came to stand by me and to read also the long inscription at which I was gazing so steadily.

The deeply cut letters in the flat stone told simply of how a twenty-year-old boy "in all the flush and radiance of youth" had left his English home with hopes high that he would make a fortune in this new world for the parents and the sisters he loved in England. But he had been struck down within a few weeks after his arrival ("Probably yellow fever," my husband observed, noting the date) and had died in a few days. This memorial had been placed here by his "heartbroken family." "Here," the inscription read, "lies buried a mother's joy, a father's pride."

I stood there for so long musing over the words that my husband asked me gently why.

I looked up at him with blind eyes. For a moment I'd been far away, my pain swallowed up in an old, old pain; so old, so long past, yet whose bleeding presence in that instant I still felt so vividly. I said slowly:

"I don't quite know why. It seems to help, somehow. I think it's just that I get the feeling"—I fumbled for words

— "the feeling of being a very small part of a very big pattern. Something that's been going on for a long time and will keep going on for a longer time. I don't know, though, why that should help. Maybe it doesn't, after all."

He waited while I puzzled over this for a moment.

"Perhaps it's partly a sense of kinship with the human race. Grief is so lonesome. Maybe it makes me realize that we're not unique and whatever it is that has happened to our child, that's not unique either . . . and less important, all of it, than we think." I stopped again. "No, that's wrong. I can't really believe that. But it all—our love and pain and the love and pain of all the others, past and present—blends into that big pattern and when you step back and look at the pattern from a distance, it seems different."

I shook my head helplessly. "I'm not saying it right. But when you stand too close to a picture, you see the details wrong—and some things look big and some small—you know how that is. But once you've gone a few paces off, it springs into different focus and blends into a whole and . . ."

I gave up. "I think I'm trying to explain something that's too big for me!"

But my husband nodded. "It's too big for most of us," he said. "But I know what you mean."

We cabled Chap on Christmas Eve. And on Christmas morning we went to the Cathedral on the square. We knelt and I fixed my eyes on the glimmering candles and there, after a fashion, I prayed. I prayed for our soldiers everywhere and I prayed that the war might end soon. I prayed for a lad very dear to us, the son of two close friends, now dead, who was in uniform in Italy. I prayed for the safety of the boy who was fighting over Germany still. And finally I pled for the life of that other boy. Pled with a God who had for me little or no substance or reality, but whose name was nevertheless a symbol of power, and who might—just possibly might—be induced to do something about this, if only He could be brought to consider the matter.

The night we took the train for home I saw a group of soldiers kneeling on the cold station platform, shooting dice. They were laughing heartily about something, and a man near us remarked admiringly:

"You can't beat the spirit of American kids! They've been waiting on a delayed troop train here for twenty-four hours, and look what a good humor they're in!"

Suddenly then my eyes stung and there was a warmth in my chest. It might be like that in the prison camp where I was still so sure (as far, at least, as I allowed myself to know) *he* was. Maybe there, too, the soldiers, in that comradeship of which he'd written with such glowing affection, managed to laugh and to snatch some fun in spite of cold and hunger and confinement.

We came home on the twenty-seventh. Friday the twenty-ninth was just around the corner.

On that morning I found beside my plate at breakfast a long envelope from Washington with the Air Force Headquarters label in one corner. The letter within explained that since three months had now elapsed, the names and addresses of the next of kin of our son's bomber mates could be released. We had written headquarters requesting this information at least two months earlier and it had been denied on the grounds of "security." So now I read eagerly, with a warming sense of kinship, the names of these strangers, wives and parents, who had shared with us more than three months of suspense.

"They won't know any more than we do," I said, "because of course when there's any news, we'll all hear at once. But I think I'd like to talk to some of them tonight."

I telephoned the pilot's wife late that afternoon, reaching her home about five hundred miles away almost immediately. However, it was her mother to whom I talked.

"Oh, the navigator's mother!" said a pleasant voice when I had introduced myself. "I'm so sorry K—— isn't home to talk to you. But she's working and she hasn't come back yet. She felt it was better for her to keep busy—she's going to have a baby and it's been hard for her—of course she'll have to stop soon, but until then——"

"I know," I said. "The suspense . . ."

"Oh!" The voice seemed for an instant to break. The exclamation was almost a sob, before the speaker caught herself. "Of course you don't know; I don't know why I should have thought you did. There wasn't much suspense for us—just two weeks. It was only that long after the missing wire came before we were notified of our boy's death. He—he was killed. A bullet in his back . . ."

Their boy—the "little pilot" Goodrich had grown so fond of. . . . "A quiet little chap," he'd written, "a Kentucky farmer, salt of the earth, solid, dependable, steady, true. Our crew is lucky." . . .

I couldn't speak. The kindly voice was still talking. It was saying that the pilot had been picked up from the Baltic Sea and was buried in Sweden. It was repeating "a rumor in a letter we had today" that the copilot had recently "escaped through Sweden" and was back at his base in England. It was adding that "we are praying with all our hearts that this means the rest of the crew are safe."

I faltered out my sympathy at last and hung up. While I talked, twilight had fallen and the room was dusky. I stood staring into a shadowy corner, both hands pressed to my cheeks, shaking. . . . Then the major had been right. Something much worse than I'd been picturing must have happened on that morning of September twelfth. Something much bloodier and more violent than just a forced landing and all the crew taken prisoners. Because the pilot was dead . . . the little pilot was dead. Picked up from the Baltic with a bullet in his back. Oh my God, why the Baltic? Weren't they on the way back to England from Germany? Why, why the Baltic? How had the copilot got to Sweden?

"Don't get frantic!" I advised myself sharply, trying to

45

still the racing, incoherent, thoughts. "Try to think!"

I tried. The pilot's wife had been notified two and a half months ago; notified that her husband was dead. But we hadn't been notified that Goodrich was dead, had we? Well, then, if he, too, had been killed when the ship went down—never mind just now where, that was something I couldn't know—wouldn't we have been advised of that fact at the same time she was? That was logical, wasn't it?

A great wave of sympathy for the pilot's family and of relief for us swept me. I dialed Long Distance again and asked for the home of the copilot's parents, in New England. The operator reported that all the circuits were busy and it might be a few hours before she could get my party; she would call back later. I was just hanging up when my husband came in, and I told him my news.

"So you see—I'm sick about the pilot—but I think that means we can be certain Goodrich is all right, don't you?"

I had snapped on a lamp. He stood looking at me, and his lips were tight. I began to be frightened.

"You do think so, don't you? Don't you?"

He answered quietly, "I don't know. I just don't know."

"B-but . . ." I stopped an instant and began again. "But don't you see? If anything had happened to him, why wouldn't we have been notified when the pilot's family was?"

"We would have been—if they'd known. We'd have been notified that he was safe, too—if they'd known that."

"Oh, don't, don't, don't!" I cried.

46

He separated my clenched fingers gently, holding them. "I don't want to be pessimistic. I don't want to frighten you. But it frightens *me* a little to see your hopes soar so high, to see you so confident—because of what it might mean for you later . . ." He swallowed once. "No, I didn't mean to say that, either. I only mean—can't you see, nothing is different yet? We still don't know. We still don't know *anything*. We still have to wait."

It was eight thirty before the Long Distance operator phoned to tell me that she was ready with my call. I clung to the receiver while I waited as if it were holding me up. It was hard to breathe. I kept telling myself, "The news is sure to be good, it has to be good, I *know* it's good. In one minute now everything will be all right; in one minute the nightmare will have ended. I only need to hold out for one minute more now—after all these months I can wait one more minute—just one more—"

And then the operator said, "Ready," and after that I heard a new voice calling, "Hello! Hello!" It was the copilot's mother.

I told her who I was. I explained breathlessly, the words stumbling a little, that just today I had received the addresses of the next of kin of my son's bomber mates. I repeated what the pilot's mother-in-law had told me about the copilot. . . . Was it true? Had she heard? Could she tell me anything? It had been so long . . .

There was a heavy silence at the other end of the line. I said, "Hello—hello!" sharply, and the voice replied.

"I'm here," it said. "Only I don't know how to . . ." It came to a halt, then went on. "My son is home. He has been here for two weeks."

"Home? In the United—?" My throat closed.

"He's out to a dance," said the copilot's mother. "Or I'd let you talk to him."

"But—two weeks! Why didn't he get in touch? Why . . . ?"

I knew why. Nobody would keep good news that long.

The voice said unhappily, "The Government forbade him. They said—they told him he must wait till after Christmas. He's writing to all of you—all the families of the crew—now. He thought he shouldn't mail any of the letters till he was ready to mail them all. It's—it's awfully hard for him."

"Oh! Then—then—the others—except the pilot—the others are all prisoners?"

The woman at the other end made a sound; a gasp—or a sob. I began to shake.

"That's it, isn't it?" I babbled frantically. "It's funny the Government wouldn't tell us, but maybe it hasn't cleared yet officially. Those things are queer, aren't they? He escaped—your son—and the rest are still in prison, and naturally he dreads to tell us, anybody would feel the same way—that's how it happened, isn't it? Oh, please——"

Suddenly I stopped. I whispered, "Tell me . . . tell me *quick*."

The voice was heavy, reluctant, when it came again.

"The news is bad. It's terribly bad. They're all gone. All except my son. He is the bomber's sole survivor."

I hung up. If I said anything I cannot recall it. I simply hung up, as I remember.

But indeed I remember little about the next few hours. I know that my husband called the number back, and asked a few questions, and left our number for the co-pilot to call when he came in— "no matter what time." And after that I think I was walking up and down the library, just walking, back and forth, twisting a handkerchief between my fingers, not weeping, not talking.

I realized vaguely that my family were around me—the boy's grandmother, his aunts, his cousin—and that friends were coming and going. I think that they spoke to me, tears on their cheeks; that occasionally someone came and paced beside me, or tried to get me to stop and lie down. Perhaps I replied to them. I really do not know.

For the first sharp, clear memory after that talk with the copilot's mother is the moment, about half past twelve, when the copilot himself telephoned; my husband took the call, and I sat on the couch a few feet away and listened with numb incredulity to what he was saying.

"Yes," he was saying, "yes, I understand you're under orders but of course we'd like to know all you can tell us. . . . Never mind the name of the country—just tell me what happened. . . ."

Thereafter for several moments he said only, "Yes. . . .

Yes . . . I see . . ." and once, "How many fighter planes?"

Finally he said, "Then he was alive when you jumped? . . . You didn't actually see him die? . . . You're sure he's gone? . . . You're—quite sure?" And then again, "I see. . . . Yes . . . Yes. . . . I see."

After a while he said heavily, "Well, that seems to be that. . . . Yes, I understand . . . Thank you. Good-bye."

He put the receiver slowly back on its hook and turned to face me. But for a moment he did not look at me. He stood leaning against the bookcase, his eyes closed. Then he opened them and came to me, where I waited, and put his arms around me.

"We have to be brave," he said. "We have to be brave. As brave"—The quiet voice stumbled, broke, then caught itself—"as brave as *he* was."

5

Briefly, the story of the way our boy had died was this: after the bomber was wounded, the four officers reconsidered their first decision to attempt to get back to England.

"We didn't want to cross the North Sea in that shape," the copilot explained. "If you go down in the North Sea, it's just too bad."

So they decided to try to escape into Sweden instead.

They were well over the Baltic Sea in sight of safety; so close indeed that Swedes standing on the banks watched the entire tragedy and Swedish newspapers wrote it up the next day, when seven German fighter planes appeared. The crippled bomber was unarmed; the guns had gone overboard to help maintain altitude. She was at that moment laboring along barely a thousand feet over the sea and quite defenseless. In this condition she could do nothing except dip her wheels in the forlorn hope that the Germans would accept her surrender. She went down with them dipped.

"They kept firing and firing," said the copilot. "The machine-gun fire was going through the ship like a sheet of water."

By some extraordinary chance, he alone parachuted out. Looking back from the water he saw his ship explode and dive headfirst, flaming, into the sea. The watching Swedes saw it, too, and put out in boats to rescue possible survivors. They picked up the copilot, unharmed save for shock, and the pilot with a bullet in his spine, dead. All the rest of the crew went down with the ship.

One part of the short story afforded my husband and me some satisfaction for slightly different reasons: the pilot, the copilot, and Goodrich had been around one hatch in the nose of the ship, after the pilot abandoned the wheel. The bombardier had gone into the back with the enlisted men.

"I told Goodrich to jump first," said the copilot. "We all

had our parachutes on. I called to him, 'Navigator before copilot,' and he yelled back, 'To hell with ceremony at a time like this—jump!' He must've been hit almost the minute I left the ship because it doesn't take anybody but one second to jump.'"

We knew that Goodrich himself would have laughed over our making a hero of him on the strength of this incident. We assumed that the copilot was nearer the hatch or at any rate in a better position for jumping, and that it was as simple and instinctive a courtesy on Goodrich's part as standing aside to let someone else go through a door first. But we felt—we still feel—that for such courtesy to function at such a time with such naturalness indicated a basic courage and unselfishness. Chap, writing from England later, said, "It was heroism at its simplest and so at its highest. He died as he did because he had lived as he had."

But whereas the boy's father glowed quietly with a deep, inarticulate pride in these qualities he had shown at a moment when a lesser man might have forgotten everything except self-preservation, my chief comfort was in the thought, Thank God he wasn't terrified—not panicky-terrified, anyway! Because terror like that is such suffering, and if he didn't feel it, then the end was easier.

It was typical of us both, that from the moment of hearing the copilot's story my husband accepted the fact of our son's death completely; while I struggled still for months not to believe it. The morning after the conversation I telephoned to the kindly major in Casualties who had talked to me before. He was sharply disturbed that I had received unofficially word which had not yet reached his department officially. He admitted that the story, as we had heard it, "didn't look good." But survivors were notably untrustworthy in their testimony, he said; not purposely, of course, but because they were usually in a condition of shock and unable to be accurate. In any event he himself had no right or power to confirm the boy's death until definite information came to his office or until at least a year had elapsed.

In the meantime we had a further report from our New York sister, the boys' "Aunt Bet" who had taken a trip to Rhode Island to talk to the copilot. The details she telephoned us were only further confirmation; and she, like her brother, simply accepted her nephew's death from there on as a fact. But I, on the slim basis of the major's refusal to confirm it, promptly set about the attempt to make bricks with no straw whatsoever, and to erect a solid mansion from nothing but mist. I cannot say that I was successful in this attempt—but at least I worked hard at it.

I pored over the maps, measuring mileage, making painstaking little marks, then rubbing them out and doing it all over again, in the effort to estimate how far the ship had been from Denmark when it went down, and whether, perhaps, Goodrich mightn't have jumped, after the copilot had left the ship, and been carried by air currents to Denmark, where he was now a prisoner.

I asked questions of everyone who would be at all likely to know, and some who wouldn't, about how far even a slight change in the position of the plane might affect the spot where a man landed when he parachuted out. I gathered eagerly stories about men who jumped within a split second of each other and reached the ground miles apart. I listened hungrily to kindly people who said, "Well, if it were my boy I'd never give up hope." And I wrote letters—heavens, I cannot even remember how many letters I wrote or to whom they all went. I wrote to the families of the rest of the crew, most of whom responded with a frantic hopefulness to any theory I might dream up for survival. I wrote to the copilot, trying to make him remember it differently, trying to make him say that it was entirely possible that Goodrich had jumped and landed on Denmark, until finally he wrote me desperately, "I understand what you are trying to do, you are trying to make Goodrich alive, and I wish to God you could, but I don't think he is, and I can't tell you so." I wrote again and again to the Air Corps and to the War Department, begging them to investigate more thoroughly, pleading for lists of prisoners from Denmark—sensitively aware that I was making myself a nuisance to busy, harried men, but driven by an urgency I could not control.

They did investigate—and would have without my letters, of course—and on March first they sent us another wire stating that our son, Lieutenant Goodrich C. White, Jr., formerly reported missing in action on September twelfth was now reported killed in action on that date near Trellingen, Sweden.

What I said when my husband came home with this wire was, "We've taken it twice—in September and December. I guess we can take it a third time."

But I wanted to cry out in desolate protest, as I sat there staring at the yellow slip, "Oh no, oh no, this wasn't what I was asking, this isn't why I urged you to press investigations! I didn't want you to hurry about proving him dead. I wish you'd waited longer so I could have hoped—just a tiny bit, anyway, for longer. Don't you see, I wanted you to prove he was *alive?*"

But they hadn't. We planned a Memorial Service in his memory, and the wonderful, loyal friends, who had been standing by us for so many months, rallied 'round again, and called and wrote and sent flowers, bless them. I sat in the quiet church and listened to the pastor who had taken him into the church at eight years and to the scoutmaster who had encouraged him to earn his various badges; and perhaps a sense of support came to me then for I did not weep nor wish to weep. Afterward we came home and I lay down for a while and my husband came, to kneel by the bed, and say, "We'll have him again, and we've still got each other and the other boy—we can go on the rest of the way, the little short rest of the way, cheerfully, can't we?" And just then, somehow, in the strange peace of the moment, it seemed possible.

But it was nothing I had thought through, nothing I had earned, that peace; perhaps it was only a brief vision of what might be. So it did not endure. It was that spring that someone quoted to me one day a sentence the source of which I do not know, but it haunted me. "The dead ride fast." Sometimes, after that, I seemed to see him when I went to bed at night, going farther and farther from me, turning his head once in a while to look back over his shoulder, but growing ever more distant and shadowy, harder for my straining eyes to discern.

In a frantic attempt to bring him nearer, I began to hunt for another way out; for some theory, any theory, that would at least delay complete acceptance of his death. I found it when I happened to run across a story of a boy first reported missing, then reported dead, who later turned up alive. I argued with my husband.

"These things do happen—they do! Now just the other day I read . . ."

And then I'd be off on the latest case I'd discovered in which a mistake had been made in a death report. My husband mostly heard me in silence, pitying and troubled.

Finally I made another trip to Washington and tried to coax the kindly major in Casualties into agreeing with me that there was still just a possibility, since Goodrich's body had not been recovered, and nobody actually had seen him die, that he might yet be found—alive. The major shook his head regretfully. The investigation before a death wire was sent was very, very thorough, he said.

"But I've heard of such cases!" I insisted. "I read—and just the other day someone told me . . ."

I was very thin now; and my eyes, my whole self, must have pleaded with him, desperately, senselessly. He answered with a sort of rough distress:

"I know those stories. Once in a blue moon they're true since nothing is infallible. I've got the figures somewhere —the number of times it's happened. About one tenth of one per cent, I think—maybe less. You'll do better to accept his death as a fact, Mrs. White."

I thanked him and left. I thought, But if it was a blue moon for somebody else—even one tenth of one per cent or less—it might be a blue moon for us, too.

Did I believe it, even genuinely hope for it? I do not think I did. Just after the war there was a story which kept bobbing up at intervals for at least a year in the newspapers. A mother whose sailor son had been lost in the Pacific not only absolutely refused to concede that he was dead, but she had decided that another boy living in quite another part of the United States, a lad whose picture she had chanced to see in the newspaper with a homecoming group of sailors, was in reality her son. For months she wrote to this young man, wrote over and over, begging him to abandon his assumed name and come home. In vain he replied denying that he was her son, offering proof after proof.

She simply repeated stubbornly, "But I know it's my boy!" and sent him pictures of the family and of her son's fiancée, pleading, "Come back for their sakes—for her sake—come back!"

Finally she went to visit him, taking the fiancée with her, and then, at last, the impact of an alien personality in its alien setting swept her dream away. She said, as she left him, "I guess now I've got to face it."

Still another woman of whom I have recently heard lost her son in a boating accident three years ago, but because his body has never been found, she still refuses to admit his death. She insists that he was hit on the head, has amnesia, wandered away, and will someday come to his senses and return. She keeps his room always ready for him and talks constantly in a confident tone of "when Bill comes home."

These are extreme cases. Not many people advance quite this far into delusion. Yet the difference between them and me, at that period of my experience, was a difference only of degree; perhaps not even a very great degree. So I think that I understand these women, and I do not believe that the mother who wrote those piteous letters to a stranger actually believed she was writing to her son, or that the mother who keeps Bill's room ready really thinks that Bill will ever use it again. Deep down inside both of them must have known clearly all the time that these were games, absurd pathetic little games, played to keep from "facing it." I played games, too, but neither did I believe them with more than just the very top of my mind. Scratch the surface even slightly and I knew the truth quite well.

Finally I stopped talking about it to my husband. Partly because he never played such games, but partly, too—I hope—because I saw that I was tormenting him almost past endurance.

"I don't know what to say," he told me one night despairingly. "For me to be the one who keeps smashing your hope—I can't take that. But I can't tell you I've got any myself. I haven't. And to watch you trying to fool yourself . . ."

I said, "I guess you're right." But something in me still kept clamoring, "He could be wrong, though—he could be!"

Along with everything else I was discovering, these days, a new sort of terror. I had never been fearful for the safety of our older son; now I was terribly afraid for the safety of the one who was left.

"You mustn't think of me as flying every day," he wrote. "Because I don't."

It didn't help. I didn't know what days he flew. I still flew every day.

SIXTEEN BOMBERS MISSING FROM YESTERDAY'S RAID! the headlines would cry in the morning newspaper, and my heart would lurch sickeningly in my breast and suddenly the breakfast coffee and toast was nauseating. If one of those sixteen was Chap's bomber, I wouldn't even *know* for another two weeks. He could be dead this minute under the waves of a foreign, far-off sea, and I'd go on getting letters and writing letters for all that time.

I'd made one effort, immediately after the copilot's report, to get him home. Sympathetic friends urged us on to it, and my husband tried to do for me what he would never have done for himself. He secured an affidavit from a doctor stating that in his opinion anxiety for the safety of our sole surviving child was endangering my health; he wrote to his senator; and after an imposing portfolio had started on its way to Chap's CO in England, he wrote to the boy himself.

"You won't want to come back before your missions are completed," he wrote. "But please do, if they'll let you. For your mother's sake."

It wasn't a fair appeal; we both know it now, and maybe we knew it then. We have both since been glad that Chap was never forced into making that painful choice—although we know that his decision could not possibly have been to return whatever it had cost him to refuse us. The CO, however, wrote sympathetically that he had no power to grant what we asked. It was only when two sons had been lost, he explained, that regulations permitted the surviving third to be returned to his home.

"But we haven't got a third son," I said bitterly. "If they kill this one, too, that's all."

Yet even as I spoke some part of me more clear than these muddled emotions was reminding me that I knew more than one couple who had lost an only son—indeed, an only child, often; and that according to such logic as mine those boys should never have been required to undertake military service at all.

And somehow, in a fog of pain and fear and dazed grief and constant anxiety, the days went past; queer, blurred days through which I moved numbly, trying with all the strength I could summon to conduct myself creditably, to imitate the steady courage of my husband, and to be a little worthy of the constant affection and loyalty of my family and friends.

Until, suddenly, it was May and the war was over. Chap was safe.

"There was a lot of celebrating," he wrote. "I didn't join in. I didn't feel in the mood for it. Peace has come too late."

But it was not too late for us, since now we could begin to plan for his return. It was not too late to bring a relief that was so blessed that, illogically enough, it made hope for the other boy spring to life feverishly in my heart again. Wasn't this sudden, tremulous happiness I felt a sign in itself? How could I feel happiness if one of the two boys really was dead? It must mean that those stubborn hopes of mine had been based on a solid intuition of fact.

So I waited tensely for news of American prisoners. I read that those in Denmark had not yet been heard from; and my spirits rose. I read, a bit later, that now they had all been reported; and my heart swung downward again. But a few hours after that I saw still another item, stating that the small island of Bornholm off the coast of Sweden was in the hands of the Russians and that probably some Americans were being held there. Excitedly I got out my well-worn map once more, and studying it decided that it was just as likely that Goodrich had parachuted down on Bornholm as on Denmark. By some sort of mental hocus-pocus, I believe that I even persuaded myself that it was, on the whole, more likely; though just how I reached that conclusion, I am unable now to remember. The point was that Bornholm provided me with a little extra time when I need not, once and for all, "face it." I assured myself that if he were there, it would probably be weeks before we heard.

I suppose I must have known how insane this latest theory was, because I was careful not to expound it to anybody. I only kept saying to myself:

"I needn't give up entirely—not yet. There's still *some* chance, still *some* hope. We might hear before the end of the summer. It's possible—we *might*."

And we did, in a fashion. On July nineteenth we received an air mail letter from Washington telling us of the receipt of a cable from Sweden. This cable, which was quoted in full, stated that the body of Lieutenant Goodrich C. White, Jr., had been recovered on July seventeenth by the Swedish Coast Patrol from the Baltic Sea, near Trellingen, Sweden, and had been positively identified.

So now no other subterfuge was possible. Now there was no other place to hide. Now I, too, had to face it fully. My enemy, Death, had found me at last, completely.

And in that hour I knew clearly, despite the strangeness

and the terror of his aspect, that he was, after all, a familiar figure. I had only pretended—a shallow enough pretense —not to know him, only pretended that I did not see his face. In actuality I knew its lineaments quite well. I had always known them. For he had indeed, as I saw plainly now, never been far away.

6

The first vivid emotional realization that comes to a human being of the mortality of all living creatures leaves him changed. It is necessary from that time on to live on those terms and to most people the terms seem too hard; therefore I am quite honestly persuaded (and observation strengthens this conviction each day) that the large majority do as I did—they escape by pretending it isn't true for as long as they possibly can.

To me, as I have said, this seemed the only "wholesome" course, and if challenged on the point I would have replied quite honestly:

"Well, what do you want me to do? Go around all the time remembering that I and everybody I love has got to die?"

An absurd answer, from my present point of view, but a sincere one, and perhaps even, as long as I held the opinion about death's meaning that I did hold, the best one—temporarily, at any rate.

Of course there are people who do not run away. Some don't because they can't; and these, imaginative, oversensitive, highly organized, may become morbidly obsessed with mere dissolution, horribly fascinated by it as Poe was. Or death may seem to them an unbearable indignity inflicted on the human race—"I am not resigned," sings Edna St. Vincent Millay rebelliously. Or perhaps their knowledge simply informs each moment, even the happy ones, with a terrible poignancy and pain because of its fleetingness. "Look your last on all things lovely every hour," de la Mare tells us.

There are others who by virtue of some innate sturdiness —and perhaps a certain lack of imagination, too—are able to look quite squarely at mortality and shrug it off, saying, "No use making a fuss—you'll go when your number's up. Just have a good time while you're here, you can't take it with you."

66

I am sure these are well in the minority; I suspect it takes a good deal of hardness as well as sturdiness to be casual about death.

I also suspect that the Stoic, with his noble but bleak acceptance, is an even smaller minority. In fact, while I admire this philosophy for its courage, it seems faintly inhuman to me.

Those who manage to achieve genuine serenity in the face of disaster and death are those with deeply held spiritual convictions (not necessarily the same thing as theological beliefs, I am afraid) and a fine, balanced ability to meet reality without dodging. To this all-too-small group, both my husband and my surviving son belonged.

I do not know just why I did not. It is not my intention to psychoanalyze myself. It would be tiresome and besides my explanations would probably be shallow and overeasy. I know that I read a great many fairytales when I was a child and that I became convinced that waving a wand was quite the most agreeable way to secure what one wanted. I know that I was very much inclined to escape into a dreamworld when the actual one did not please me. I fancy that my first encounter with death, probably the loss of a pet, horrified me deeply for some reason and that I arranged from then on to be as unaware of it as I could possibly manage. But certainly none of this is at all uncommon. Indeed, I must repeat that I do not think my attitudes were uncommon.

It did, at any rate, take me a year of struggle even to begin to understand what my husband and Chap seemed to know immediately and intuitively, without making any effort to discover it; that the first step in intelligent adjustment to grief is just the simple, complete acceptance of what has happened. Later each one of them, when talking of those first weeks after the copilot's report came, expressed this in his own way. Chap said:

"At first all I could do was just take it on the chin. I sort of squared myself to meet it—that was the best I could manage."

And Goodrich Sr.:

"I had to tell myself, 'Here it is. You knew it might happen and now it has. You've got to take it, and if you let it get you down and keep you from doing your job, you're yellow.' "

I was desperately eager to conduct myself with courage. I reminded myself constantly that I had no right to act as if I were the only person in the world with a trouble, that many others were enduring the same pain. I flogged myself on, after the first few weeks, to keep up with all my usual activities. I bought new clothes, went to parties, started back to the beauty parlor, took little trips, and formed the habit of keeping our big house blazing with lights every night so it would not look lonely or sad to friends passing by who knew that there was sorrow inside.

All the same, however much I assured myself that I was trying with all my might, I was actually not taking the trouble well, and I knew that I was not. I was like a man who, sorely wounded, clenches his teeth and by main force

68

keeps on his feet, but finds it quite beyond his powers to walk steadily. I looked a little worse each day, in spite of the beauty parlors. I might go through with the proper gestures, but they were only gestures, and no one who knew me could be at all unaware of that fact. I recall that once my sister burst into tears and implored me, please, not to smile!

My husband, watching me anxiously, attempted to talk to me about "accepting things" but I did not understand what he meant and flared into something akin to anger.

"That's foolish! What else can I do—since July nineteenth? Maybe I wasn't as absolutely sure as you were before, but I am now."

He shook his head.

"No, you were absolutely sure before. You knew from December twenty-ninth on—we all did. But you didn't accept it then and you don't now. You're in constant, violent protest against it—you're tearing yourself to pieces inside with protest all the time."

I answered in a sort of sulky despair, "I still don't know what you mean. Am I expected not to feel grief?"

"No. Do you suppose I don't feel grief?"

I supposed nothing of the sort. I was silent, ashamed. He said gently, "Do you remember that story about Margaret Fuller and Carlyle? She is said to have flung her arms wide and cried, 'I accept the universe!' and when this was quoted to Carlyle, he commented, 'Egad, she'd better.' Well, he was right, she'd better, but I've always thought she wasn't as foolish, all the same, as he made her sound. It isn't so easy to learn that one had better."

For an instant, I saw dimly what he was trying to say; saw that if one persists in beating one's head against a stone wall, it is seldom likely to be the wall that gets broken, only the head. I asked humbly:

"How do I learn to accept it?"

And he answered, after a moment, "That's a hard question. I'm afraid I don't know how to answer it. I guess I'm in the same fix you've been in when you've tried to tell me how to relax as thoroughly as you do—how to go to sleep at the drop of a hat as you can." He grinned. "You always say, 'Just let go. Just take it easy. Just *relax*.' And about all I can say now is 'just accept it.'"

He thought a little. "What you have to do is to start with the fact. You have to stop trying to get around it. You have to stop going behind it. You have to quit rebelling. You have to give up always iffing and whying. Just start with what happened—and adjust from there." His smile was a little rueful. "That's the best I can do. Not good enough, probably. But you might try."

I looked at him helplessly. I felt that I didn't even know how to start trying. I couldn't go on from the fact because I couldn't get past it. It stopped me over and over.

I, who had always so prided myself on "being wholesome," now lived over and over in imagination all that had happened on September twelfth, seeing it from the first

70

moment when the bomber was injured, clear to the last when the waves closed over hissing flames . . . so often, indeed, that I sometimes had the confused feeling that I must actually have been there myself. I seemed to know, not as one who has heard but as one who has lived, all the details of that last tense half-hour of my son's life.

A hundred times I went over all the possibilities that might have prevented his death. If only I'd begged him not to join the Air Corps . . . if only he hadn't been transferred to a new crew . . . if only the ship hadn't tried to escape into Sweden and the boys had simply all parachuted out and given themselves up . . . if only the fighter planes had been five minutes later arriving . . . if only the ship's surrender had been accepted . . . and so on and on in what is, of course, just about the most futile type of thinking in the world. For if it is foolish to worry before the event, as had always been my hearty creed, how much worse than foolish to keep on fretting after! There are no more "ifs" after the event.

Also, in all this frantic racing to and fro of my thoughts I was making an unwarranted assumption; the assumption that if things had not happened the way they did, they must have happened a better way. Forgetting that we never know what might have been, but only what was.

One sensation which I had felt strongly when Edwin died was with me constantly now; a stark sense of incredulity. What had taken place that September day seemed to me fantastically impossible, and no matter how coldly my mind gibed, "Idiot! He was no different from any other flesh and blood, no less vulnerable to bullets," I couldn't bring my emotions into line. Indeed this sense of incredulity was so intense that sometimes when mind and heart were especially weary and drained, I used to think:

"I believe I could learn to take it if I could ever really believe it."

I recall riding through autumn beauty in October sunshine one afternoon, that fall of 1945, and saying to myself:

"Suppose, right now, when I got home this afternoon, I should find by some miracle that everything was all right again? Suppose the two boys were in the side yard playing catch and the dogs were lying around on the grass and everything was just like it used to be. Even then, even then, wouldn't the scars of these dreadful months still be there?"

And suddenly I knew they wouldn't, for I would forget. I would forget because it would seem simply natural for things to be as they had been. It was the way they were now that seemed unreal. Yes, I would forget—or rather I would remember only as one who has awakened remembers a bad dream, shivering a little and saying, "Heavens, what an awful dream!" but knowing that now that it is over it doesn't matter any more and that even the memory will soon fade and grow misty.

Chap's safety continued to be the bright spot of our days,

after May. He did not come home until September fifteenth; and all that spring and summer before, his letters showed, if just I'd been able fully to understand them, the slow but mature progress of his own adjustment.

"I'm not fooling myself," he wrote, "I know things will be different from here on out. And I know in some ways the hardest time is still ahead of me, when I come home and begin to do alone all the things we planned to do together. The better times I've trained myself to look forward to and live for during these war years just aren't coming, not in the particular way I dreamed them. But life is still good and I promise you I'm going to be all right. I'm like a man who has lost a leg. He knows the stump must heal. His leg is gone—but he knows that someday he'll learn to walk on the wooden one."

He went on a trip into Devonshire alone that spring, spending most of his holiday on a bicycle as he and his brother had done when we were all four together in England and France in 1938.

"The moors looked exactly as they ought to have looked," he wrote, "and I expected at any moment to see the Hound of the Baskervilles emerging with dripping jaws from the mists." (Conan Doyle's thriller had been a great favorite of both boys in their early 'teens.) . . . "So you can see that I tried to do and to see all the things we would have done and seen together if he had been with me. And most of the time I felt as if he actually were with me, just there riding

73

along on another bicycle beside me. I think it will always be like that for me. He'll be in everything interesting I do, everything beautiful I see, all my life for me."

I read this with an uncomprehending envy. The boy who had died over the Baltic that day was not in beauty for me. He was not in anything except my painful memories. He was gone. That was why beauty hurt now, because he no longer had a share or a part in it in my mind.

Later still Chap wrote something so profound and far-reaching in its implications that I wonder if even he himself fully understood all it meant when he wrote it; if it was not one of those flashes of insight which come to people sometimes almost "from the blue." Certainly *I* did not even begin to comprehend what such a feeling might mean for one and do for one till long afterward.

"There is something," he wrote, "that I'm finding out, and that is that when I feel saddest, why it's then that I seem to have lost him. But when I'm playing on my fiddle, or just laughing and talking with the boys, he comes back to me."

I read and reread these letters with much pride and little understanding. (Exactly as, later, I was to realize that I had read some of the other boy's letters with little understanding.) And I continued to watch my husband with a wistful wonder. How did he go ahead as he did, as he had from the very first, doing an enormously complicated job, taking no time off, asking to be excused from nothing? Most of all how did he continue to put just as much heart and just as much interest into it now as before, quietly cheerful, not even flogging himself into doing it? While I forced myself to do everything I did! Why, he hadn't even lost flesh—with me looking more like a gray wraith each day!

Sometimes I tried to tell myself, "It's because he has a job in which he believes wholeheartedly." But I believed in that job as wholeheartedly as he did and had a share in it which I wasn't adequately meeting. Besides this, I had my own work; and if it wasn't as important as his, still it was mine, and till now I had always enjoyed it and felt a little sense of achievement when the checks for it arrived. I wasn't doing that job, either, these days.

Maybe at this period I would even have liked to think that he cared a little less than I did. But I couldn't. I knew better. For I knew what his sons had meant to him; knew the deep, inarticulate pride he'd had in them, knew the way they had loved to laugh and play together, knew the satisfying, inexpressive, masculine companionship among the three.

One evening I tried to find his secret.

"Just knowing how to accept—that couldn't make all this difference between you and me, could it?" I asked.

"I don't know." He paused an instant and then said, with the hesitancy a reserved person feels when speaking of something that lies very deep, "You see, I don't believe people die, except physically. He's not here and I miss him more than anybody knows. But I believe he's alive somewhere."

"You mean spiritual life," I said, after a moment, drearily.

75

For spiritual life seemed so very hazy and ghostly to me that even if I had been sure I believed in it, it wouldn't have helped much.

He frowned.

"You make it sound—awfully dim. I just mean life. I guess you'd call it spiritual. But it's real."

I was silent. It wasn't real to me.

"I suppose one thing," he went on, still hesitantly, "is that I settled what I believed about this years and years ago. I went through rather a confused and unhappy time till I had, but finally I knew where I stood. To me it's the only rational belief, the only one that makes sense out of the universe—and I believe the universe is sensible."

"I just—never thought about it much," I said faintly.

"No. I know. Maybe your temperament was sunnier and you didn't need to. I don't know the reason. But for me nothing was worth while till this was settled. My job wasn't worth doing and even you and the boys didn't make life worth the effort."

He finished simply, "I believe he's alive. I believe I'll see him again. I believe we'll laugh together once more."

I could only look at him helplessly.

Sometimes I tried to pray. After all, I had been raised within the church. I had never dreamed of bringing my own children up in any other way. I knew the vital reality that religion had been in the lives of both my parents. But I knew it as an onlooker, and the church to me meant a set of desirable ethical concepts. I had never even asked myself why they were desirable. And now there seemed to be nothing of any substance to which to cling. Still, remembering the peace that prayer had often seemed to bring my mother, I tried to pray.

After my husband was asleep, I'd slip downstairs to the library, where the boys' books and records were, where the great bronze bust of Beethoven brooded over the silent piano. And there I'd plead:

"Show me a way out of this, show me a way not to have to stand it, it can't end like this, it can't!"

And the "prayer" would usually close with childish, bitter accusations.

"You don't care! You don't help! You don't answer! You don't do anything! I don't believe there is a You at all."

Yet here I must record one curious little point; that is, the sensation that came to me as I hurled these accusations, of a certain perverse pleasure, as if I were hurting Something or Someone too patient to strike back. It was the bitter satisfaction one gets, when badly hurt oneself, from hitting out and hurting, even if blindly, in return. A child may hurl such invectives at a parent—"You're mean! I hate you!"—knowing that he is powerless and his parent all powerful, but in his puniness aware that at least he can inflict emotional pain on one who cares.

I suppose that even this very poor substitute for prayer, even these hysterical pleadings and foolish resentments, wildly expressed, were a certain sort of prayer; were, perhaps, a very short, staggering, first step. Not that the step seemed at the time to take me anywhere at all—except perhaps a bit deeper into the darkness where I wandered.

Finally I'd steal upstairs, stiff and drained and uncomforted. I hadn't found an answer to anything. But one thing I knew, from July nineteenth on; I knew it more fully every day, knew it with every drop of my blood, at last, and every fibre of me; that everything ends and everything dies.

That was the real element of despair in my grief. It was not so much that the boy was no longer with *us*. I had never expected that he would continue to be so, once he was adult. This adjustment I had made gradually and painlessly, —even contentedly—as the children grew; and I had always rather resented being told that we were going to be "awfully lonesome" after they had left us. I did not think that we would be lonely, my husband and I, as long as we kept each other. Of course I looked forward to the fun of watching our grown-up children fulfill their destinies; of seeing and having a small part in their family lives. But I knew that our places must be in the background of these destinies, and I felt no sadness or rebellion at this. Because I had already ceased to think of the boys as peculiarly our possessions in the sense that small children belong to parents, and I contemplated their adult estate with a pride and depth of satisfaction which more than made up for the loss of the old, intimately dependent relationship.

Ah no. It was much less that this son of ours was not with us than that he seemed to be nowhere at all. He had disappeared as utterly as if he'd never existed, as if he had been only an impossibly lovely dream we'd had, not flesh and blood. This is the real tragedy, the real blackness, of grief.

So my sorrow was greater than sorrow for any one individual, however beloved. It was equally for a lost illusion of happiness, for a lost picture of life. I ached these days with a terrible, cosmic pain of pity which seemed to embrace all mankind. Poor mankind who must so surely lose all that is dearest, who must so surely die! The sight of happy people who went along blithely not realizing (as I had, as I had) hurt me more acutely than the sight of unhappy ones now. The happy ones had still so much to learn—so much to lose; and the lesson and the loss were so terrible.

I had always believed in the happy ending. I had even avoided stories that ended unhappily, dismissing them with my favorite, "That's morbid!" This despairing conviction which now possessed me that there was no happy ending for anybody, that for everybody nothing waited but grief and the blackness of dissolution, made the world appear to me an almost intolerable place and life itself too much to ask of any human soul.

And the only dim comfort I could find was, after all, a horrible sort of comfort; the thought that it didn't matter much, really, whether the brief journey was pleasant or painful, since the end was always the same and came so soon.

7

Chappell had written from England, during those last tedious months of waiting that were, he later declared, worse than combat, that he was determined to get home for his birthday, September sixteenth, and for the World Series. He reached us, as a matter of fact, on the fifteenth of September, 1945, and he did not go East to college for his professional training until January of '46.

The months between were something we all needed, but it was inevitable that for the boy they should be difficult, I am afraid. He did not express this, nor did we discuss it, but we all knew it. The home was much changed. Most of his close friends were scattered. He missed his brother and he missed, I suspect, those deep friendships men make in time of war. He was troubled, too, about the years that the war had stolen from his preparation for his career. He was more committed to his chosen field than ever, since it was what he and Goodrich had planned to do together, and utterly determined not to yield to discouragement.

He bought a car in December and I drove to New York with him a month later, planning to return by train after a short visit there. As we rode, that chill January day, I looked at his young profile beside me there above the wheel, graver and more mature now under its sweep of bright curly hair, and asked him a question.

"Do you believe that Goodrich is still alive? Somewhere? Or somehow?"

He hesitated. "Why, I'm not very imaginative, you know." (A notion he has about himself which definitely libels him.) "I don't picture it concretely. But yes—I do believe it." He turned his head for an instant. "Don't you?"

The road was smooth and shining before us. The trees against a steel-gray sky had that strong, delicate grace which summer covers and winter discloses. "They're incredible things, trees, aren't they?" Goodrich had said once wonderingly. "Lovely in summer, of course, all lush and green, but even in winter . . ." He'd stared up at the dark, intricate tracery, trying to find words. "It's a perfection of line—not a bit of adornment, just pure beauty of line—and it's oddly satisfying." He'd stopped, as he so often did, half ruefully, unable to find the phrase that conveyed just what he meant. . . . For an instant he had come back to me vividly in the small memory. I bit down on my lip and said, after a moment:

"I suppose I don't quite know what I believe. I keep thinking how he loved everything about living, everything he saw and did. And then I think how cruel it is that he had so short a time of it, that he had to miss so much. I feel—I feel so agonizingly sorry for him because he had to die."

"Sorry for *him?*" asked Goodrich's brother. His tone was surprised. "I don't get that. Why?"

"Why?" I echoed, surprised in my turn. "How can you ask? When he wanted so much to live and to come back to everything—and he never came back? When he missed so much? Love—marriage—parenthood—"

I stopped. I was remembering how I'd turned sick with pain only a few days ago because I'd passed on the street a blond young Air Force officer, a slim little girl clinging to his arm and looking up at him adoringly, while he smiled down at her. But I didn't want to explain to this other son of mine, still so young, that curious sense of guilt which a parent feels to be still alive, so unfittingly and improperly alive, when his child is dead. I didn't want to explain that one's own gift of life becomes almost hateful when one's child is denied it. Perhaps he couldn't even have understood, yet, how wrong, how cruel, how almost treacherous it seemed that I, who had already had so much of my turn at living, couldn't have died for my son. What, I'd asked myself fiercely, are parents for? Well, it's a very old cry—"Would I had died for thee, oh Absalom, my son, my son!". . . My other child was shaking his head, frowning a little.

"I can't think of it that way at all. His death was *our* tragedy. Not his."

"Not *his?*" I was genuinely bewildered. "You're telling me you don't think it was a tragedy for him that he had to die?"

"The minute of dying might have been. I don't know about that—my hunch is it wasn't, but I don't know. But being dead can't be. That's our trouble."

"I just don't see what you mean," I said helplessly. "Why do we call it the 'supreme sacrifice' then? Why does even the Bible say there isn't any greater love than for a man to give up his life for his friend? If dying isn't a tragedy for the person who dies, why do we all, everybody, feel like that about it?"

Chap, who like most men gets a helpless feeling when called on to explain himself to a woman, tried again.

"Of course he wanted to live, Mother. Everybody normal does. Staying alive has always been a problem and the race couldn't have survived, I guess, if people hadn't wanted and tried very hard to do it. When you give up what you want most, it's a supreme sacrifice, isn't it? But all of that is the way you feel *before* you die."

"I still don't see . . ." I began; and stopped, for suddenly I did see.

Why, of course. While Goodrich was still alive he'd passionately wanted to go on living. Like, as Chap said, any normal individual. We're made that way and, as he'd also said, there was a good reason why we had to be made that way. We, and everything else that lives. That is, if it was conceded to be at all important that things continue to get born on this planet. And apparently it was important since such constant effort went into assuring it.

But afterward—well, afterward, Goodrich was either still alive or else completely dead and gone. It had to be one of the two. If he was still alive, it was only logical to suppose that his life was likely to be on better terms, since it was further along in the plan of evolution—whatever that was, and if there was one. Anyway, I thought, it was rational to assume simply that if there was another life, it was better, because more advanced, without getting myself too involved at this point. So much for that. But if he were completely dead—what then? Well, nonexistence was painless. It was folly to be "sorry" for him in that case, because there wasn't anybody to be sorry for. . . . I winced, and realized immediately how right Chap was—it was *me* his nonexistence hurt.

So the only way I could reasonably be sorry for *him* was

84

to suppose that he was still alive and didn't like the conditions of his new life, was homesick for the one he had left. And perhaps that was exactly what I had been feeling, without quite analyzing it.

I said aloud, slowly, "If he is alive—I wonder if he wishes he were back again—with us and his friends and his dogs. I wonder if he likes the way he is now as well as he liked the way he was then."

Chap turned his head to look at me an instant and smiled a little before his eyes went back to the road.

"I think," he said lightly, "that I'll have to tell you a little story. It's one I heard Deems Taylor tell once over the radio. He said he had a little red wagon, when he was a kid, that he was very fond of, and one day it occurred to him that he had never seen a grown-up person playing with a red wagon, and he burst into tears. His mother asked him what in the world was the matter, and he explained between his sobs that he didn't want to grow up because he was afraid that when he was grown he couldn't play with his wagon. She laughed and tried to comfort him. She told him there wasn't any reason at all why he shouldn't play with his wagon if he liked, no matter how old he was, that no one would prevent him. 'You can play with it as much and as long as you want to,' she said. He cheered up for a second and then began to cry again, harder than ever. She asked him what the trouble was *now* and he explained between sobs, 'But I'm afraid I won't *want* to!' "

I remembered that story a few days later, on the train. Remembered it with a sense of uneasiness as if even now, though I'd laughed and said I understood, there was a point I hadn't fully grasped.

Chap was beginning the long road he must travel toward his professional degrees now, the road postponed by war. This Christmas the house and yard had bloomed again with colored lights, because he was back, and there'd been a tall Christmas tree, and holly, and poinsettias, and all the bright glitter and bold colors which had so delighted the other boy in past years.

Now it was over. And I realized that the deep, listless depression which had seemed to engulf me as my train pulled out after I told him good-bye at the station was due less to the fact that he was gone and I missed him (though I did, of course) than to the other fact that for months I had been straining toward just one point: "He's young, and he's been through so much—he mustn't find us or home too different, I mustn't let it be sad for him." Now, having used all my strength to reach and pass that point, I seemed for the moment to have none left, and wished only to sink down and go no farther.

Nevertheless, I must go farther. And suddenly I knew that if I did not exactly want to, I wanted to want to—which did indicate desire, of a degree. Strange how persistently vital life was. For even now I realized, with some deep part of me, how it stirred and clamored underneath the pain. I could even recall one afternoon, waking from a short nap to the familiar surge of misery, and sitting up on the bed to

86

hurl a crazy defiance at the boy for whom I grieved. "I'm tired of thinking about you all the time! I didn't think about you all the time when you were alive—I forgot you for hours and hours at a time! Why do I have to think about you all the time now?"

There were other people I loved, other things in which I was interested. Something in me rebelled against this constant preoccupation with just one person, just one thing. Yet at the same time it seemed to me that this was like saying to a man bleeding to death of a wound in his right lung, "But your left lung is all right, and there's nothing the matter with your heart or your stomach or your liver—why don't you put your mind on *them?*" How could you? Your attention was fixed, almost perforce, on the area of pain.

Across the aisle from me a charming red-haired child of fourteen was chatting gaily with a very pretty mother. She had come across one of these so-called personality tests in a current magazine and was reading the questions aloud and answering them with giggles, in an effort to rate herself.

" 'Do you enjoy the prospect of meeting strangers or do you shrink from it?' " she read, and replied immediately, "I like it fine, I think it's exciting. I'll bet that shows I'm sociable and gives me a good grade. Oh, here's one." She paused. " 'Are your sex impulses wholesome and normal?' " She knit her brow a bit over that one. "Well, I'm not sure —what do you think, Mother—are they?"

"They seem absolutely all right to me, Carolyn," her mother replied calmly, and, quite satisfied, Carolyn went on to the next question.

At that moment the other woman's eyes met mine across the aisle and we exchanged smiles. We were strangers, but they were intimate smiles, charged with the tenderness that candid youth awakes in most women, and as I turned to the window again my heart felt warm and amused. In the brief human contact I was, for an instant, wholly myself again. Then I thought, Suppose she died, that pretty child —how dreadfully the memory of dear, funny little things like this would hurt her mother! God, don't let it happen, don't let that nice woman find out how bad it is! And the moment was spoiled as I seemed to see the placid, pretty face across from me all changed and wan and distorted by tears.

"But why must I be like this?" I was demanding of myself passionately the next moment. For today I seemed to know deeply—shrinking from the knowledge, almost rebelling against it—that in a grief which continued, after more than a year had passed, to so cloud and overshadow all of life, something was very wrong. What I did not know was how to change anything—and yet hold, as I felt I must, everything he had ever given me, remember everything he had ever meant to me.

I had often been told "Time heals." But to me (perhaps quite wrongly) that meant "Time dulls." It meant a sort of forgetting. So it was an answer that, for myself, I rejected.

For if the radiant young figure must grow less bright before comfort could come, its outlines blur into mist as it retreated farther and farther down the silence of the years, then, as far as I was concerned, that was purchasing comfort at too high a price.

It might, I thought, be very well, it might even be the best solution, for someone who was younger, of whose life the one who was gone was not so vital a part. But for me it would mean losing such a very large slice of myself that I could not believe I would ever again be a complete person.

It was then that I suddenly thought once more of Chap's little story; and now I seemed to know clearly the answer *he* had been trying to give me. He had been saying, in effect, that of course I could not picture or understand Goodrich's activities now any more than the child in the story could picture or understand grown-up activities—all of which appeared to him immeasurably inferior to playing with a red wagon; but that I could take it on faith that those activities were as far beyond the things Goodrich had once known and done as the joys of adult life were beyond the joy of owning a little red wagon.

I could see the point academically. But if it didn't seem real to me, I couldn't make it so, could I? If I tried to force it, it would be just fantasy. And fantasy wasn't real.

It was here that I remembered, almost with reluctance, that once, for a very short while, it had seemed real. It was an experience which I had discarded completely in bitter disillusionment later, and then had tried to forget. Because the memory of all I'd thought I had, all I'd so soon lost, had hurt so much.

That evening my husband and I had sat up late in the library, listening to the radio and reading. At midnight he took the dogs out for a brief caper, and I went about the lower floor, snapping off lights. The rooms were filled with roses and a vase of red ones stood beside the boy's picture. All the lamps but one were switched off now, and I paused an instant before the photograph while I waited for my husband to come in, looking at the young, smiling face.

I cannot explain what happened then. It is even hard to tell, for actually nothing did "happen." I saw nothing. I heard nothing. It was simply that as I stood there, suddenly the boy was beside me.

I had not been calling on him; I had been calmer and quieter of spirit than was common in those days. Almost one might say it came at a time when I needed it less than usual. And it seemed to come entirely from outside myself and with an utter authenticity.

It was as startling as the appearance of a person one has supposed to be thousands of miles away, and I am helpless to find words that convey its complete reality. It was as warm, as vibrant, almost—in a queer way—as *solid*, as ever his presence in the flesh had been. Perhaps I can express it best by saying that it was only later, after the sensation itself had faded, that doubt came; and it was only later that it could have come. For at the moment itself, in the glow of assurance that he was there, it simply was not possible to disbelieve. Literally no more possible than it would have been at the times when I had seen—heard—touched him.

Under the impact of that strange and lovely conviction, I spoke aloud in a voice of breathless, delighted amazement.

"Why, Darling! You're here," I stammered. "You're here, aren't you?"

Then, still with no words, but as strongly and positively as ever his words had come, I felt his pleasure. It came in a rush, as if a glowing, tingling current of air charged with some vital electric quality had enveloped me, and it conveyed a sense of happy relief as definite as a joyous shout. "Well, thank Heaven—at last!" it cried.

With that, I began to weep, tears of sheer, stunned happiness, and of a relief that was close to ecstasy. My husband found me like that when he came in with the dogs; and I told him what had happened—and was still happening— and saw his own face light with pleasure.

"Can't you feel it, too?" I asked. "You can tell he's here, can't you?"

"Not just as you're feeling it. But I believe it," he said. "Why not? It doesn't seem strange to me."

We walked upstairs, and the boy walked with us, an arm about my shoulders as he used to do. And I fell asleep whispering to him, "Don't leave—don't ever leave—please stay!"

That night I dreamt vividly of walking with him on the banks of a green lake beneath a brightly blue sky, and I woke cheerfully and normally, as I'd almost forgotten how to wake in past months, and went downstairs making eager plans for the day.

When did I lose it? I hardly know the exact moment. I only know that as the day wore on, slowly, slowly the warmth began to leave and the chill to creep back. I struggled against it with a sort of desperation. I tried to recapture the magic by force of sheer determination. But it was no good. Inexorably the curtain which had parted for a brief enchanted glimpse was sliding back into its accustomed place, its dark, impenetrable folds once more hiding all which might—or might not, how did I know now?—be behind. Useless to try to seize it and hold it apart; as useless as to try, when wide awake, to keep the loveliness of a dream that is slipping away. In despair I gave up the attempt and bitterly accepted the penalty of having mistaken illusion for reality.

"It wasn't you!" I cried to empty space which gave me back no answer but the hollow echo of my own voice. "I don't know what it was, but it wasn't you."

Yet here on the train today, remembering, I found myself thinking strange thoughts. Did one ever stay on the peak of any emotional experience? Even that warm, outgoing gush of sudden pride and delight in the persons one most loves—which visits one sometimes and is among life's loveliest moments—was always sure to ebb. But did any reasonable person ever say thereafter, "How sad! I find I don't really feel that way about them at all!"?

Suddenly then I recalled a man for whom an experience akin to mine had lasted. He had come to see me a few days after the copilot's report, a close family friend, an executive with a rare combination of vision and practical common sense. And he had told me, sitting there by the couch where I lay, that after the death of his first child, he had gone off alone and had passionately cried out one question:

"Tell me—will I ever see her any more?"

Then, as he waited, the answer had come, clear and strong and definite.

"Yes, yes, yes! She is alive and you will see her again. Be sure."

And with that (he went on) the most complete certitude had flooded him with peace. His heart was still sore for the sight and sound and touch of his baby, but the blackness and the wildness of grief was gone.

"I went on missing her," he had ended, "but it never was again like it had been at first. Because always after that I knew. I've known ever since. I still do."

Lying there, with one hand over my eyes, I'd listened and wondered dully why he had supposed such a story would bring me any comfort. And I'd said, at last:

"Forgive me—but don't you think you gave yourself that answer? Just because you wanted it so badly?"

Then I'd taken my hand down and looked at him and seen that he was shaking his head.

"No," he'd said. "I was afraid I couldn't make it real to

you. I'm sorry, because it was real. I think the answer came because I asked in utter sincerity and held myself open honestly to receive whatever might come."

So for him it had endured. What then if mine had been lost because of some failure within myself?

Suppose, I thought, that when I felt the shining interval leaving me, I'd still believed that once I'd had it! Suppose I had said to myself that afternoon:

"Ah, I couldn't sustain it. My senses are earthbound and have shut the realization of him off again. Never mind. Because I *did* know it last night, he *was* here, and if I keep mind and heart open and ready, perhaps once more all things will converge, as they did then, and he can make me feel his nearness again. But even if he can't, it happened once, and I know he isn't far away."

Suppose I'd said, and felt, that. Would all these months between have been different—perhaps, perhaps?

And at that, sitting there with eyes closed on the rushing landscape outside, the most desolate sense of loss and regret imaginable swept me; almost a sense of having forfeited, no worse, pushed off and denied something lovely and dear.

"You might have taken a chance on its being true!" said a small Voice inside my brain. "It wouldn't have hurt you just to have taken a chance, would it?"

I retorted passionately, "It's dumb to be tricked by desire into foolish credulity!"

And the Voice, which was Me speaking to Myself, replied:

94

"Is it any dumber to be fooled by overcredulity than by overskepticism?"

"I haven't got the sort of mind that can make itself believe something merely because it would be a nice and sweet and comforting thing to believe!" I said.

"Why, that's exactly the sort of mind you *have* had for years and years!" retorted the Voice. "And now you've swung so far the other way that it seems you've got to keep yourself from believing what's nice and sweet and comforting only because it *is* like that. Nice, sweet, comforting things are sometimes actual, you know."

"This one isn't," I muttered stubbornly. "This one is fantastic."

"Oh, fantastic!" the Voice answered. "You mean that you don't understand it, that you can't explain it. But as to that —there are so many things you can't understand or explain. It doesn't follow that they're unreal and fantastic."

"Oh, what's the use of this?" I cried. "It doesn't get me anywhere. The plain fact is, I don't know what I believe or whether I believe anything. All the nice comfortable feelings I once had about things have vanished. I'm all at sea. I'm not even an intelligent agnostic. I'm only hopelessly mixed up."

"In that case," said the Voice, and now it had begun to fade, "in that case, isn't it about time that you began to try to think things through? Isn't it about time to make at least an effort to find out where you stand?"

It stopped. I opened my eyes and blinked at moving trees and fields. Mentally I called after that vanishing Voice: "Yes! I agree! High time!"

And suddenly then I felt a little of my weariness and my lassitude leave, and a little spark of interest flare up. As if, crawling painfully through a dark tunnel, I had seen—still faraway and dim—a tiny gleam of light.

It might be just an illusion of strained eyes and heart. It might not mean daylight ahead. There might not be an opening, and beyond it green grass and blue sky and flowers.

There might not—but on the other hand, there might.

It was at that instant that faintly, ever so faintly, with little of the joyous assurance that first experience had held and less of its surge of rapturous relief, I seemed to catch what sounded like—well, what did it sound like?—a distant shout of encouragement?

No one stood beside me this time, an arm about my shoulders. Rather I felt, trembling a little, that perhaps one standing on a hilltop had called a heartening "Halloo" to a traveler lost and floundering in the thickets and marshes at the foot; a "halloo" that pointed a path up, and out, and cried, "Don't lose heart—the path is there—keep searching, you'll find it. This way, this way!"

I hardly knew so much as how to begin. Yet in that instant of turning my face toward that hilltop, of barely, barely hearing that cry, I took (though I did not realize it then) the first hesitating step. For at least now I wanted to find the path. And there is no way to rescue a person who deep within his heart, even if quite unknowingly, prefers to remain lost. Such a one will not see a path, whoever points it out; will not hear a voice whoever calls; and such a one, albeit unconsciously, I had been.

8

A few years ago an old friend, who is also distinguished in the literary world, urged us to gather together and publish in a small volume some of Goodrich's letters which we had shared with him. We considered the idea, a bit wistfully; and gave it up, a bit reluctantly.

The letters are naturally valuable to us. We feel that they reveal an ardent, gay, lovable nature; an unusual sensitivity to beauty; and a deeply practical substratum of hard common sense running solidly beneath these traits.

But many other young men have written such letters—letters that are intelligent and aware, full of idealism and eagerness. These gain a poignant quality when the young hands that penned them are still, but we felt that there ought to be a better reason than that for publishing them. We realized that we had not thought of them as extraordinary while he lived. We enjoyed them, we felt a glowing sense of pride and satisfaction in the development they portrayed; but this was a highly personal reaction felt in equal measure of the letters we received from our other son. It would not then have occurred to us that anyone outside of the family circle and a few close friends would be particularly interested in reading them. That judgment was more dispassionate than any we could make now, so we feel it had better stand.

The story, however, of any individual's adjustment to grief is bound to be affected in part by the quality and nature of the person for whom he grieves. It was a very important element in my own case, since things I had not fully realized or understood in our son when he was with us emerged with startling clarity after he was gone, and finally profoundly influenced me. Toward this fuller understanding, the rereading of his letters contributed much; and from these letters I quote later a few paragraphs which revealed with new vividness some aspects of his personality.

Of course I know that the commonly held opinion that

we tend to idealize and make impossible saints of our dead has a measure of truth; but it is half a measure. For death reveals as well as beclouds. And we are not always wrong when we seem to discover new beauties in those who are no longer physically present. Once the small rough edges that are always there in every human contact are gone—those obscuring human irritations which mortals put upon one another almost helplessly, whether they will or no—the individual may very well have a chance to emerge more clearly and definitely for what he actually is.

I suppose that how one feels about a statement like that depends partly on whether one holds that what a man actually is, is his best self. In any case, it may not be a test, but is a noticeable fact, that even if one does not believe it about other people, one practically always believes it about oneself, even if unconsciously; and betrays that he does by saying, when he deviates furthest from his own standards, "I wasn't myself that day." He even says it when he is merely ill or unhappy; "I don't feel like myself." Something stronger than any opinion he claims he holds is deeply convinced that he is most truly himself when he is at his best.

If an observer stands quite close to a picture, he often sees discordant details and harsh colors which seem to disappear when he steps back a few paces, leaving a satisfying, harmonious whole. Actually they have not disappeared, of course. They have merely lost importance because that whole is seen to be beautiful, and it is the whole that matters. Always provided, of course, that the picture is fundamentally of sound construction to begin with; otherwise quite the reverse might easily be true, and what dazzled in its details could look sadly changed when the entire aspect was viewed from a wider vantage point. Again, if the picture is still in process of being painted, it is impossible to judge it adequately; it is constantly changing, certain things being added and certain others subtracted. It is only when it is completed that one sees it as a whole.

Death brings the opportunity to look at a portrait from that further, clearer position and to see the completed picture.

Quite honestly I do not believe that I had much tendency to idealize my son's memory. I did not need to; he had satisfied me as he was, and I was even—as I have a way of being with those I love—quite fond of his faults. Indeed, at a later period when my ideas about death were beginning to alter drastically, I passed through a somewhat absurd phase of resentment at the thought that his new life must be so immeasurably wider, so crowded with dazzling opportunities and interests, that he himself must change and grow greatly in the living of it. I did not want him to change; and I was jealous lest growth mean growth away from *us*. I wanted him exactly as he had been—quite ignoring the fact that even in the more limited period of earthly existence people constantly change and grow (or else deteriorate, that being, apparently, a law of life) and that, in any event, one's children do not stand still and halt their development at any time of their lives, merely to suit their parents' foolish wish to keep them as they are!

It was, therefore, rather in spite of myself (almost as if from outside myself something or someone was exerting silent pressure) that certain attributes of Goodrich's began, as I looked at him from this different vantage point, to emerge with new clarity and sharpness. And more and more, even with a certain reluctance, it began to seem to me that it was these aspects which were most vitally and truly of the essence of him, himself, and therefore must be what had predominantly survived his physical death.

This is my story; I am not free to tell the experiences of others; but this much I may say—that for half a dozen other people close to the boy it is precisely these same facets of his personality that now stand out in the brightest, boldest colors, it is in these terms that they oftenest think and speak of him. I have watched this happen; I have watched the almost incredible influence it has had and continues to have, the amazing changes wrought by its silent power, in personalities other than my own, with wonder and something approaching awe.

So what I shall say about him in these next few pages, and such paragraphs as I shall quote from his letters, will be partly concerned with these qualities which, as I have said, have emerged with this sharper clarity for us who loved him, since that day in September. Not for a moment must it be supposed, therefore, if I select for quotation—for example—those letters in which he writes of what beauty meant to him, that he was always writing like this. I know now that life, without this excited apprehension of beauty, would have been for him so dull as to be almost valueless; he said as much to me once when he was about sixteen, angry at the indifference of some friends, with whom he had been strolling, to a gorgeous sunset sky. "They didn't even care! They hardly looked! My gosh, if I ever get that dull and blind, I hope I die!" . . . thus unconsciously echoing Wordsworth. But it is quite equally true that he also had all the normal interests of any normal boy of his age, and he wrote of these interests at length; baseball and tennis and football and Boy Scout badges and swimming; his dogs, his friends, his brother, the girls he dated. He was highly expressive; he liked to talk and write of what he was thinking and doing and seeing, and probably did do this in more detail than the average lad. He loved long discussions and arguments with congenial souls about all sorts of matters, abstract and concrete.

"I should have been an ancient Roman of the aristocracy," he sighed one night after a group of four of us had sat on the edge of a mountain, watching the lights in the valley and the dark line of the hills beyond it, and talking and talking and talking till long past midnight. "You know —hanging around the baths and just discussing things all day long!"

I ran across one letter not long ago which I had largely skipped at the time I received it—from sheer boredom, I fear—and almost guiltily, beset by that irrational but natural human feeling that now every written word of his is of great importance, found myself skipping still. Stopping over in Washington he had seen an unusually exciting baseball game, one which later became historic, I am told, and he went back to his hotel and wrote us a play-by-play description of it. I might add that the other two males of the family did enjoy this one. Another I was never quite able to complete instructed me at length and in detail, with the somewhat pontifical arrogance of extreme youth, on how to listen to the *Missa Solemnis,* which I was shortly to hear. I believe his brother still regards this letter as some sort of model listening-pattern. To me it appeared stuffy. Letters from the weeks he spent at summer camp frankly boast of athletic prowess—"I'm really awfully good at volley-ball"— and those of the Army period are characterized by the candid references to "chicken" that seem to be an inevitable portion of the soldier's correspondence. In one of these he refers morosely to a certain officer whom he describes as a "nasty little pot-bellied major," who is, he declares, "a horse's rear end if there ever was one." There was one relative who occasionally visited in our home, an individual whose standards not only of conduct but of expression were irreproachable and rigid, for whom I always deleted parts of these Army letters when I read them aloud.

I am trying, in short, to say that I wish to be careful not to give the impression that I am presenting Goodrich as a creature made of special clay; that would be both a fatuous and untrue picture and would—if perchance he looks over my shoulder as I write—irritate him profoundly. Moreover I do not believe that those spiritual qualities in him which we who were nearest him now discern so poignantly could influence us as they do, had he not been also, like his brother and thousands of other boys, a healthy, outdoor youngster, happily adjusted socially. It is against the background of his entire personality that these special traits must stand out.

It is true, however, I am sure, that every individual has his own unique and shining quality, if only it can be seen and developed; Goodrich's, it seems to me, was a plus response to life and all its experiences and sensations. A temperament like this is almost certain to be outgoing, perhaps a little aggressive, and adventurous; his was. I have indicated that this plus response showed particularly in his reaction to beauty, an ardent reaction in which his whole heart was involved. Everyone who came at all closely in contact with him felt this. It was more than a year after his death that we started off on a cross-country trip at dawning, with the fine colored friend—who came to us when the boys were practically babies and has been our constant support and help ever since—in the car with us. Suddenly we saw that she was quietly weeping.

"It's the sunrise," she said. "There's no use trying not to think about him all the time when everything keeps on reminding you—why, he'd have run two miles to see a sunrise like that!"

"I know," I said. "And do you remember how he used to

absolutely lose his head every springtime, and spend all his spare hours—till he'd actually get worried about his school-work and his practise—running around with a camera, trying to get colored pictures of dogwood and tulips and azalea and wistaria and crabapple—and always groaning over the results because they never could capture the beauty of the originals?"

We laughed then, a little tremulously, and recalled that it had been the same in autumn; and that ice and snow had also enchanted him; and that moonlit nights had made him a little fey, so that he could not stay in the house, but was apt to go wandering down the road at two in the morning, taking a reluctant, crossly protesting member of the household with him if he could manage it, alone if he could not.

This response of his to beauty was indeed so deep that it held (and this is one of the things we see with that new sharpness of clarity now) a curiously mystical quality. In some manner beauty, whether of sight or sound, opened to him the door of another world. I am aware that this does not express quite what I mean or quite what he felt, but I simply know no other way to say it. George MacDonald, who has coined so many strange and lovely phrases, spoke once of one "haunted by the scent of unseen roses." Goodrich was haunted all his life, I think, by this fragrance of unseen roses; and there were times when, for a rapturous instant, he seemed to catch an authentic glimpse of the secret garden itself, and always the passing of the moment left him wistful. "It makes me sad," he said one night as we watched a moonlit scene of such sheer magic that it seemed unreal. (He was in his middle 'teens.) "It makes me sad because tomorrow it will be gone and I'll forget it." Then, after a moment he added, "But even if I forget it, I don't really ever quite get over it."

Among his letters I find one written when he was about thirteen, the second summer of four that both boys spent away at a summer camp in the North Georgia mountains. He was describing an overnight hike his group had taken.

"It was"—he wrote—and I reproduce the spelling which certainly shows no great scholastic precocity—"a long climb, a pretty hard one, too, becaus that's a big old mountain. We climbed for three and a half miles and most of it was pretty stepe. Finelly we got there and picked our camp site and built a fire and cooked supper, and boy, it tasted swell. Afterward we chose our place to sleep. But what a night! It was glorious. A feild of broomstraw dotted with low pines on a very high spot. A strong wind sweeping it and the sky full of brilliant stars. I made my bunk close to the fire where I could watch the embers. They kept dying down and then being fanned into flame again by the wind. Then the moon came out and thin clouds blew across its face without hiding its light only just for a minute at a time sort of shadowing it and though I was warm and comfortable it was so beautiful and exciting and awe-inspiring that I stayed awake a long time enjoying it."

It was a few years later that he tried to describe a sunset

and this time he expressed in somewhat more mature terms that sense which beauty evidently gave him of being thrillingly close to the borders of a different, an unseen, country.

"I'm rather excited," he wrote. "I've been seeing the most incredible sunset. It had been raining and late this afternoon it suddenly cleared off, and I give you my word everything turned gold. Not a hard, glisten-y gold, but a soft, orange-colored, mellow gold. The sunlight lay on the ground in pools that looked all thick and liquid, as if you could take a spoon and scoop it up. Then the air itself began to fill with an apricot mist, shot with gold that quivered and gleamed. All this time the sky in the west was simply indescribible." (He still had not learned to spell one hundred per cent; in fact, that continued to be a weak point.) "A sort of fiery gold background like flame all crossed and streaked with lines and bands of rose and green and violet and pale yellow. In the east it was all one color and what a color. A blue you had to see to believe, it was so deep and brite. And hanging right in the middle of that distilled blueness was a slim little white crescent moon. The whole thing made you feel like you'd stepped right out of the ordinary world into another dimension."

After he began to fly (he always insisted that the real romance of flying came when one was alone in a small plane with an open cockpit), he wrote of cloud formations, of riding down a blue lane between banked-up masses of black storm clouds, of the colors of the earth as seen from above, of the gleaming pale silver of rivers and the fairylike radiance of cities at night. Always, as he talked of these things, there was the same aura of joyous excitement, the same half-unconscious insight into something behind the appearance of things to a lovely reality beyond, shining from the words. This reached its height in a passage in which he tried, with a feeling of evident inadequacy, to share with us the experience of seeing the Pilot's Cross.

"Did you ever," he wrote, "hear of the Pilot's Cross? It's a familiar phenomenon but I never happened to see it till the other day. You know we must fly above or below the cloud banks. I was flying quite high and beneath me there was a thunderstorm going on. Then the sun began to shine and suddenly there below me I saw something that took my breath away. It was a cross—a shadow of my plane—entirely enclosed and encircled by a rainbow. I begin now to understand why flyers so often grow mystical. Alone up there with so much loveliness around you and beneath you, you know you're drawing close to Something great. I can't describe it, but there's a sense of something wonderful just around the corner, and a feeling that one of these days you're sure to find it. Your blood begins to race exultantly and you want to laugh out loud and—oh well, I'm saying it poorly but it makes living a very great adventure. I don't know—perhaps I'm trying to express something too big for me—but just for a little you feel as if you know, dimly, what the whole darn business is about and as if dying is going to be a very great adventure, too."

On the whole it may be that he came closest of all to the

"feel" of that other world in great music—for music was the genuine and the biggest passion of his life. Passages that express this can be picked almost at random from his mature letters.

"I hardly know how to tell you about the concert," he wrote from New York, just a short while before he entered the Army. (He had, indeed, already enlisted and been accepted for the Air Corps and was only waiting his call.) "When it was over Aunt Bet and I simply sat there and looked at each other, neither of us saying a word. I left the hall in a daze and I've been like that ever since. What he does with a piano is beyond belief. You can talk about his wonderful singing tone, his lack of percussive effect, his marvellous technique, and it's all true enough. But it leaves out the biggest thing of all. It leaves out that deep tenderness, that spiritual glow, that glimpse into infinite beauty which could only come from a great mind and heart that is, in turn, in touch with some power more than human. Do I sound gushy? Well, truly in the presence of art like this, what can one do but pray? It's getting truer and truer that I never listen to great music without becoming keenly aware that it stems from a power much bigger than the man who is performing it—and even bigger than the man who composed it."

Then he added—this vigorous, normal, young man who had always managed his life with poise and common sense and balance, who was fundamentally such a hardy individual—something so deeply mystical that even now, today, I am barely beginning to understand what he must have meant.

"So," he wrote, "that at times I have queer thoughts— and I wonder whether Beethoven's music, for instance, must not somehow have found a channel through to the world even if Beethoven himself had died at birth. Now," he concluded, "I've taken off into the wild blue yonder quite far enough, don't you think? So goodby for this time."

9

But if Goodrich was a mystic he was, as I have intimated, a practical mystic. For me that is important. Because if my new awareness of his spiritual qualities has increased my own spiritual perception, so has my knowledge of his sturdy realism kept me, in turn, firmly in touch with actuality. This was, perhaps, a balance I personally needed.

He had a mind that, for all the richness of its inventive

imagination, worked clearly and logically with an almost mathematical coherence and consecutiveness. He had a passion for classifying and cataloguing, and he methodically card-indexed, from ten years old on, practically every possession he most treasured; his sheet music, his records, his books, his Kodak pictures. Even today we use those meticulously neat card indices in finding a sheet of music or a picture we want. One of the last things he did before flying overseas was to recheck all these records. Then he arranged his books on the bookshelves alloted to him, and admonished me with a hint of severity, "Don't lend them to anybody till I come back. Read them yourself if you want to, of course, but please put them back exactly in the same places. I want them to be *just like this* the next time I see them."

As a child even the wildest of his imaginative fancies had to find expression in some concrete way. Daydreams alone were never enough—though when *I* was a child they satisfied *me* completely. But if he was living in an imaginary country for a season, as frequently happened, he had to draw a map of it. More than one, usually, elaborate and exact, showing cities, mountains, rivers, seas. If he was exploring a jungle, he took time off to go to the piano and pound out, and afterward jot down, a weird series of chords which he called "The Dance of the Cannibals." Every mental activity had to be translated into a material achievement before he was satisfied. He had, indeed, a passion for facts. Even facts that seemed intensely dull to me were interesting to him and he collected them and made notes about them. "This book," he solemnly inscribed of an especial volume in an elaborate catalogue he made of his favorite books (he was then eleven) "has two hundred and fifty-six pages with an average of thirty-two lines to each and every page and an average of eleven words to each and every line, being also six inches long and one and half inches thick and haveing twelve chapters and ten ilustrations."

This sometimes seemed to me a queer streak to be found in such an ardently imaginative individual. And equally queer, at times, did I find his vein of almost tough philosophy in a nature as sensitive and as intuitive as his. Just before the Air Corps called him, I remember, we were talking of a young man who was a "conscientious objector" and had refused military service on that ground.

"He's perfectly sincere," said Goodrich. "But he's fuzzy-minded. Doesn't think straight."

I protested indignantly that this was unfair, and he shrugged.

"Well, look, what do you suppose is going to happen to him? He'll probably be sent to a CO camp somewhere in the West—I know two fellows who're there now—and he'll cut down trees to build ships and be working just as hard for the war as I'll be."

"Well—yes. But maybe he feels it's a different sort of work. I mean, maybe he'd say he was willing to do almost anything for his country except kill for it."

"If that's what he thinks," said Goodrich, a little impatiently, "then it certainly proves he's fuzzy-minded. All he's saying, whether he knows it or not, is that he isn't willing to *be* killed for it. He does kill for it, when he helps the war along."

"But——"

"There isn't any but," he said. "I guess I feel a little strongly about this. I don't like hearing you say, 'He'll do anything for his country but kill for it.' It's not fair. I'm telling you right now that I shan't take one bit more responsibility for the bombs I'll have to drop than he's got—or than you have, either. You pay your taxes, don't you? No, you can't get off that light—you can't say, 'I'll manufacture the gun and the bullets, and I'll pay for them, but here, you fire it! I just can't bear to hurt anybody!'"

"I see all that," I said, a little disturbed. "But still, I'm wondering—well, tell me if you were quite honestly and quite sincerely a conscientious objector, just what *would* you do at a time like this? How would you solve the problem? What would you *do*?"

He waited a moment before he answered.

"I don't know what I would do. Maybe I'd dodge the question by going into a medical unit and telling myself I was helping repair the damages of war."

"And you think that would be dodging?"

"For me it would. I said I didn't know what I would do if I were an honest pacifist—but I know what I ought to do, if I were also a brave man."

"Well—what?"

And he answered, "I ought to refuse to pay taxes, for they go for the war effort. I ought to refuse to cut down trees for ships or do any war work at all. I ought to travel up and down preaching my convictions till they crucified me."

Once, when he was home on one of his infrequent leaves after he was in the Army, I remember speaking of a friend who had recently lost her daughter, and with my voice a bit choked I read aloud to him a part of her latest letter. It was a despairing letter and a bitter one. The writer said she had lost her faith in God entirely. Never, so long as she lived would she pray again. She had prayed earnestly for her child's life—and God had let the girl die at sixteen. How could you believe in prayer any more after that? How could you believe in the kindness of a God who'd let such a cruel thing happen? If there was a God, He wasn't a loving one, and she didn't want anybody ever to tell her so again!

Perhaps Goodrich was a little too young to enter into the agony behind the wild words; they roused in him—to my surprise, for he was usually sympathetic—something curiously like anger.

"She didn't lose her faith," he said scornfully. "She never had any. Or if she did it was a funny sort. It never seems to have got disturbed by the things that happened to other people's children. God was there and a very nice, kind God till *her* child died. If it'd been her next-door neighbor's daughter, He'd still be a nice, kind God."

116

I protested that even if this was logical, it was rather a harsh judgment on a brokenhearted woman.

He shook his head. "I still think folks ought to use their minds—even if they're brokenhearted. It can be done—some do. You know that favorite little tale of yours about the man who said he wanted to ask the Sphinx just one question—was the universe friendly? Well, I can't answer that question—but one thing I do know, that it's dumb to answer it just in terms of whether things go to please *you.*"

It was perhaps partly this sturdy philosophy which enabled him to go from a civilian's life, concerned chiefly in the latter years with music, straight into the extremely rigorous training of an air cadet, apparently without strain. The first time I visited him at an airfield I protested that the discipline and the training seemed to me unnecessarily severe, and he promptly contradicted me.

"No it isn't. It makes plenty of sense. We're civilians, most of us pretty soft, and they've got to get us whipped into soldiers in double-quick time. This is about the only way."

That was another sense in which it seemed to me that some of his traits were oddly contradictory; the fact, I mean, that he was an intense individualist, and yet had an instinctive respect for discipline and authority. He never had a teacher with whom he did not "get along"—he preferred the "strict ones"—and he fitted into Army discipline with almost a minimum of "griping." Visiting him once after he

117

had won his wings, I was quite indignant at some new ruling that seemed to me highly unreasonable.

"I don't really see why you boys put up with it!" I fumed. He sent me an amazed glance. "What else can we do?"

"Well—you could get up a petition—protest . . ."

He groaned. "Chap's right—women oughtn't to talk about the Army, they oughtn't to open their mouths about it!"

"But what's the matter with that suggestion?"

"Nothing," he said with heavy sarcasm. "Nothing at all. Just mutiny. And mutiny in wartime, which makes it sweeter."

After he went into combat that adventurous streak of which I have spoken undoubtedly kept it from being the shock it might otherwise have been to a nature essentially tender and sensitive. For it was both of these; he had never been able to bring himself to hunt—though it embarrassed him to admit it—because the idea of killing any harmless animal was painful to him. "I'm a sentimental guy," he said once, almost ruefully. Danger, however, had always stimulated him. (As a matter of fact, he had a much greater dread of illness than of violence.) He enjoyed climbing an almost perpendicular cliff, while I stood shivering at the bottom; he adored crawling around on his stomach through mountain caves I was certain would collapse on him; and getting caught in a car on a slippery, unpaved, winding mountain road after dark in a wild thunder-and-lightning storm was only an exciting experience, not a frightening one. I have seen him, in moments such as these, with his cheeks flushed and his eyes shining— and I am sure that is the way he looked in the last instants of his life.

However, after he had written twice of "the thrill of combat," I grew troubled.

"I can't find you in that phrase," I wrote him. "You who never would even go hunting because you didn't like to kill any living thing! I know you have to fight—but you don't have to like it."

He replied tolerantly, "Don't get all steamed up. You surely can't think that when I spoke of 'the thrill of combat' I meant I enjoyed dropping bombs on people. Of course I don't. Sometimes I look down on the lovely countryside over which we are flying and I think of the people who live in the cute little villages and fancy them looking up at our formation and wondering where we're going to drop our load of hell and death today, and it isn't nice and I have to stop—*quick*. You must, if you want to keep your sanity, and I certainly do plan to keep mine.

"No, all I've meant to say by that phrase you dislike is that in the actual moments of combat when there isn't any time for thinking at all, there's a tremendous excitement. I suppose there is just something in us all that responds to the exhilaration of danger. In that sense combat *is* a great thrill and will be a great memory. But if you tell me it's a memory and a thrill a man is better off without, I certainly won't argue the point with you. At any rate, you needn't be afraid I'll ever get hardened to human suffering, because I imagine if there is a danger, it's the reverse."

But it was not, after all, just the obviously dramatic and exciting things that stirred his sense of adventure. All the little experiences of living, too, were charged for him with a mysterious, vibrant pleasure so that a picnic on the grass, a walk in the country, a good conversation with congenial people became an adventure. He was an ardent admirer of Proust; his treasured Proust volumes flew overseas with him—and came back later without him. He had written many notes on the margins of the pages, and one of these reads, "How often have I felt this beauty of which he speaks, a strange, sharp, beauty: Felt it suddenly in things which were in themselves quite commonplace. As if I suddenly saw them from a new angle or plane."

I suppose that a part of this was the heritage of his youth. He seemed to sense himself, toward the last, that the world might not always be quite the shining place he had found it for all his years. His birthday occurred a month before his death and he wrote at that time:

"Well, I've spent my birthdays in a good many different places, haven't I? It's nice to remember, now that I'm so far away, that I was home on leave for the last one. And I wonder where the next one will be! Anyway this seems a good time to say one thing that I think you already know; that my life up to now has been perfect. Whatever the years

120

ahead hold, I guess I couldn't really expect them to be as unclouded as the ones in the past."

But it was not altogether the heritage of his youth. For Edwin dying in his forties and my mother at seventy-two had possessed that same unquenchable enthusiasm for living during all their days.

A nature like this gathers, of course, a great richness of sensation from almost every experience. When we took the boys to Europe in 1938, our crossing was unusually smooth. Nobody was seasick; not even I, who need little excuse to be. Some days later in London we had a visit from an American friend who crossed on the next voyage of the same boat—the *Queen Mary*. He described vividly the horrors of an extremely rough voyage; pianos rolling across the salons, everyone seasick, the ship in a turmoil. When he had gone Goodrich sighed deeply.

"Some people," he said, "have all the luck. Why couldn't ours have been like that?"

"You're crazy!" I said indignantly. "It would have been awful. You wouldn't have liked it a bit."

"Now Mother!" He grinned at me. "He's already had enough fun just telling us about it this afternoon to make up for every bit of the bad part. And he'll tell it about a hundred times more in the next twenty years."

Goodrich did not really like the Army; few civilian soldiers do, I suspect. But he found a great deal to compensate in that experience, too. He wrote from England that he'd been

121

actually "homesick" for Tampa—"I had such a good time there—I got amazingly fond of the place." And once he wrote, "Of course I'm living for the time when I can come home and be with the people I love doing the job I love. We all are. But there's a lot that's good about being in the Army, too. I've made wonderful friends. And anyway, it doesn't hurt a fellow like me brought up in a University atmosphere to find out that the man who fixes his airplane is not only just as smart but probably a whole lot smarter than he is."

Only once did he ever mention to us directly the possibility that he might not return from combat. His father and I had visited him at one of his flying fields. The brief weekend was over. We had had an early dinner together and driven back to the Field where he was due by seven o'clock. Now we were lingering for the last few moments, and in the front seat of the car together, the boy between us two older people, a lovely sunset sky ahead of us, we chatted; when suddenly Goodrich, a little line between his brows, asked a question.

"Listen, you two . . . if I got bumped off in this business —would you mind terribly much?"

It was such a boyish, almost childishly expressed question! Across him we looked at each other, and it was I who answered, lightly.

"Well—I expect we'd mind quite a lot, Honey."

I smiled at him, but he did not smile back. Instead I saw, my heart turning over, that there was mist in his eyes and his lashes were wet. He blinked them impatiently and spoke almost violently.

"But don't you see? That's what I can't take. That's what makes a coward of me when I think about it. I've had such a swell time always—more fun already than the average person gets in a lifetime—maybe as much as any one person deserves. I'd like to have a lot more—I expect to, too, of course—but . . ."

He stopped. Neither my husband nor I seemed able to speak. And in a moment he went on.

"I'm just trying to say everything is okay, for me. Whatever happens it's all been fine and it's okay. But you—you two—"

He stumbled again, then finished in a rush.

"You know what I mean, don't you? I just want to know you can take it, that whatever comes you can take it, that's all."

I was still speechless. It was his father who answered him steadily.

"It's been fine for us, too. We can take it."

He looked quickly at me, and I managed a nod; it was all I could do, but apparently it was enough. I felt the tension leave the taut young body beside me, saw his whole face relax beautifully, and he smiled.

Some moments have a trick of impressing themselves with especial vividness on visual memory. I think that still the way I oftenest see him is the way he looked when he waved us good-bye a few moments later. The sky had deepened to flame now; he had kissed me and given his father a brief hug and left the car. But we still sat there, facing the gate, watching him till the last possible moment. And just inside the gate he turned to look at us again.

Behind him were low, very white buildings and bright green grass. His tall young figure, hard and streamlined from the months of training, was outlined for an instant there with almost startling definiteness against that bright sky. He had taken off his cap and the wind ruffled his fair hair. He raised the arm which held the cap, smiled at us radiantly, and called gaily, "Good-bye!"

When I see him like that, I somehow always link the picture with something else; a tantalizing fragment of conversation, a few words which I heard him say on his last short, forty-eight-hour leave before he flew overseas. I do not know what preceded those words; those who did hear the full conversation do not remember. But they come back to me again and again and I seem always to be just on the verge of fully understanding them.

In the library with friends and family, he had been having one of those lively discussions in which he delighted. I had been in the dining room arranging flowers and now I came to call the whole group in to dinner. Goodrich was leaning forward in his chair as I reached the door, his cheeks flushed and his eyes very bright.

"But in that case," he was saying eagerly, "in that case, don't you see, it's always possible for a man to transcend himself!"

10

It seems necessary at this point to repeat that if I had been unique in my attitude toward death or my reaction to grief, then this account would be just a case for a psychologist's handbook, not of any significance to the ordinary individual who would be expected to respond to these situations in the ordinary manner. But I was not unique; I was not even unusual; and the anatomy of grief, as I came to know it, follows a pattern all too familiar.

For if those who face death, for themselves or those they love, with poise and common-sense acceptance and a measure of cheerfulness instead of with shivering horror and actual panic—if these are few, why fewer still are they who regard it with hope as perhaps the gateway to another life; yet fewer those who possess a genuine faith that survival is *true*; and fewest of all the ones who believe that any continuing companionship with their beloved dead—of any nature or degree whatsoever—is possible.

Even quite honest, practising Christians who know that belief in immortality is one of the basic affirmations of their creed, are frequently entirely unable to bring their emotions into line with what they sincerely claim as their convictions, when it comes to death; and apparently dread it as greatly for themselves and "sorrow without hope" as desperately for those they love, as the unbelievers.

This difficulty in making the intangible and the invisible seem real is perhaps rather peculiarly one of our age. We call it "materialism" or sometimes "secularism" and a great many books and articles have been written about it, explaining it, attacking it, even defending it. All the reasons as to why and how we got this way have been rehearsed so frequently that we are, perhaps, a trifle tired of them: the rapid advances of science which have made life here and now so dazzling, so comfortable, so exciting that we don't wish ever to give it up—the earlier methods of science which for a time accepted nothing as truth that could not be proved by exact measurements or other concrete means —our worship of this exact science and our growing dependence on its methods to reveal ultimate truth—all these things and many others have been said again and again.

They have been quite true, and they still are to a large extent, but less and less so. (Indeed, the physicists seem to me these days to talk in a manner considerably more "mystical" than the preachers.) The age of materialism has passed its climax. But I was a child of that earlier era. I would certainly never have admitted at any time in my life that I was a "materialist"—and I do not think I was; but I had grown up under a system which took it for granted, and it was in the air I breathed and consequently in my very blood and bones. I was paying for this now.

I faced this block in myself along with some other things, after that trip to New York. I faced, for instance, the fact that somewhere on the road in this past year I had lost, together with other losses, my picture of myself. For heretofore, while never unaware of many failures and errors, I had taken it for granted, without thinking much about it, that I was an integrated and a fairly adequate person; one who was, on the whole, equal to life and did not "take things hard." Now, as I tried to look honestly at myself, it seemed clear that if indeed I ever had been this kind of person, I was no longer. In fact, I was a "problem."

Reason told me that I was undoubtedly a painful problem to my husband; I suspected that it was highly likely that I was a problem to the rest of my family and to my patient friends; and I knew exceedingly well that I was a problem to myself. It is one thing to have problems and quite another to be one. I was neither integrated nor adequate these days, and I "took" nearly everything "hard"— especially if it bore any relation to the interests of my husband or my surviving child. I was appalled to discover that trivial disappointments or backsets that had never bothered me before for either son, that had been taken as a matter of course or laughed off, now upset my balance completely for this one child who was left with us. And it puzzled me. I could not understand why grief should have all these undesirable by-products. I'd often read that it "ennobled"; it did not appear to have "ennobled" me.

If self-examination is honest, it is seldom likely to be very pleasant for most people. And by self-examination here I do not mean self-centered introspection, that constant in-turning of all one's thoughts which, while it certainly produces a very unhappy person, apparently does hold a sort of terrible pleasure; I mean something quite different, the shrinking, reluctant, ruthlessly honest effort to see one's self clearly, and to evaluate one's own motives, purposes, opinions and character without benefit of any rosy spectacles. This is an effort almost sure to be painful, and not many of us make it. Oh, we meet ourselves face to face occasionally at some bleak moment, during a sleepless night or when we wake at dawning, and dislike what we see—but normally we escape from the sight as quickly as possible without stopping, in our dismay, to examine closely.

It was this effort which, plainly, I must make now. There may be some question about the wisdom of taking a machine apart to examine its component parts as long as it appears to be running well; there is none when it has ceased to function satisfactorily. It then becomes important to find out why.

In my case the obvious answer—one you may be sure I promptly made—was that I had experienced a great grief. The trouble was that I could not convince myself that this answer went deep enough. I had had a severe blow; granted. But what I needed to discover was why I had come so close to disintegrating under it.

In the painful weeks of self-scrutiny that followed, the answers—for there were more than one—began to emerge. I knew, finally, that all my life I had feared and hated and dodged the idea of death, without once ever facing that fear, and that especially since Edwin died I had been in headlong flight. I knew how great a part of my "poise" and my "steadiness" had been based not on clear-sighted courage, but on the determinedly fostered delusion that nothing could possibly be allowed to go permanently wrong for me or those within my inmost circle. And I knew that I had never possessed any religious convictions with substance, or any faith strong enough to support me when I most needed its help.

I realized fully now that in losing my son I had also lost that lovely and impossible land in which I had managed for so many years—God knows how—to dwell, and I clearly saw how important a factor this loss was in my inconsolable grief. But this did not make me regret the vanished clime less—and in fact at that time I did not know what to do about any of my new realizations.

One which I rebelled against most bitterly, yet into which I was finally forced, was that long-continued, paralyzing grief—grief which makes the memory of the past a pain, destroys the joy of the present, and takes away all anticipation of the future—is wrong; is perhaps an actual sin. Against this growing conviction I protested almost angrily. Wrong for a mother to grieve all her days for a bright young life cut cruelly short? I demanded angrily. And something within me answered inexorably:

"That is dodging the point and you know it. Of course it isn't wrong to go on missing and wanting the absent ones you love. That is something to be felt in your heart and borne with dignity and patience and courage, and not to be dramatized or sentimentalized over. But that isn't what I am talking about. I am talking about a crippling, wrecking absorption in the loss that shuts out everything sweet and happy—and *that* is something else entirely."

That this sort of grief was wrong I found, at last, by the most positive and practical test I could devise: the results it had had. I was now, I saw shrinkingly, a more selfish and self-centered person than I had ever been in my life before, since my mind was fixed always on my own pain. About this time I read a story in which one character remarked that grief was just self-pity—we felt sorry for ourselves because we had lost something we wanted to keep. This struck me disagreeably at the time, and still does. I think it is untrue and rather cruel to characterize grief as "just self-pity." But as in so many remarks of that nature, there is just barely enough truth to make it sting. Grief is not self-pity; but it may easily involve self-pity—and often does.

I was not only a more self-centered person—I was a less useful one. That was because all my strength went into the keeping up of that "front" and there was none left over with which to plan or do constructive things. I did not have very much strength anyway—for there is no fatigue (none at least that *I* have ever experienced) like the fatigue of grief, and I woke more weary than I had gone to sleep. Perhaps I did not have much real interest, either, though I tried to deny this. Certainly I was a much less healthy individual, physically and mentally.

And oh, very, very certainly I was a far less pleasant one to have around—in fact, just plain not any more fun at all for anybody—with my haunted, shadowed eyes, and my strained smile, and my forced, artificial attempt at "brightness."

I kept telling myself, as I squirmed and twisted under these admissions that the judge within me was unduly harsh; that actually I had tried, extremely hard, and that grief was normal and natural. And in a measure I was right. I *had* tried, and grief is indeed normal, so normal that the absence of it in time of loss would be rightly felt as inhuman; indeed most psychiatrists agree that it is better, psychologically, to let this natural outpouring of sorrow have its way . . . at first and for a while.

But here again I actually knew, with that small part of me that was able to hold itself aloof from my emotions, that I was evading. What I had to face, quite simply, was the fact that a year of bitter grief had caused a definite deterioration in me as an individual of worth to those who cared about me, to society, and to myself. Natural or not, this was undesirable; and the only common-sense conclusion was that no matter how much I felt I was entitled to grieve, or how "hard" I thought I'd tried, I'd have to learn a different way of expressing grief, and have to try harder— or perhaps, again, differently—if I didn't want the deterioration to continue.

I came to this conclusion at least a dozen times, balked at it, backed off, and was dragged back again, before at last I consented to it. And the deep reluctance with which I finally did so eventually taught me another dismaying fact; I did not want to conquer my grief—I hugged it. Perhaps I had to some extent substituted grief for spontaneous, joyous affection; in any event I found that I was convinced that to give it up would be to lose some part of him. Therefore holding to it became an office of loyalty, a proof of great love.

"You got to want to feel better," my brown little "second" maid said gravely to me one day. "That's the way it was with me."

She has one of the richest personalities I have ever encountered, largely because her whole life has been spent in service and love for others and she has received a great deal of love in return; and the mature, wise philosophy she has developed is something she has carved out entirely for herself. I admire her tremendously and I listened to her respectfully.

"When my oldest died," she went on, "it came at a pretty hard time. I'd just lost my husband and there were four littler ones than her—she was just eight—and I didn't know what I was going to do anyway. Then she died and it seemed like I couldn't stand it. She was so bright and cute and always saying, 'You won't have to work like this when I'm big, Mama, I'll take care of you good then.' I went down to ninety pounds and I got so's I couldn't even take decent care of the other children, I just didn't seem to care."

She paused and I asked with tremulous eagerness, "But what pulled you out? Because you haven't forgotten her —that was eighteen years ago and you still talk a lot about her. *What did?*"

"I prayed a lot," she said. "And *she* helped me. In some ways it's right handy, having a special angel of your own in Heaven to help you."

She looked at me and saw perhaps—for she has a quick intuition—that I was looking back at her rather blankly;

133

so she added, "But what I was going to say—when I did get to feeling better, seemed like I didn't like it, seemed like I couldn't hardly let myself feel better. I'd say to myself, 'Am I forgetting her?' and then I'd go to the trunk and get out the little white dress and the little hat with a blue ribbon she wore when she joined the church and I'd get myself all upset again. And what I mean is, you won't feel better till you get to *wanting* to feel better."

"Yes—but how do you want to?" I asked helplessly.

She answered, "You've got work to do and you don't think she'd be so proud of her mama's letting all her jobs go, and you find out you don't have to feel bad all the time to remember her."

If the time had not then come when I could accept all of her insight ("it's right handy, having a special angel of your own in Heaven to help you"), part of it at least was clear: "You find out you don't have to feel bad all the time to remember her." With a vague memory of something else that bore along this line, I hunted up and reread a letter of Chap's from England; and although I still could not understand, I began faintly to discern what he had meant when he had written, "When I feel saddest, why it's then that I seem to have lost him."

And now I could even see that underlying this appearance of loyalty in clinging to grief there might be a deeper disloyalty. For shouldn't the net effect of a beautiful, radiant life on the people who have had the privilege of living closest to it—those whom its owner most loved—be altogether good? To make it specific, shouldn't *I* be an individual of much more worth, of richer, finer substance, than I could have been had he never lived?

In the past I had felt that this was true. I had felt that in a sense I grew up and started to become a real woman when he came; and that because he taught me what a selfless devotion was, I loved the others most dear to me more selflessly, too. Was I making it all untrue now, nullifying it? And in the name of loyalty to him?

Eventually I saw, almost with horror, that this "loyalty" of mine had led me to a final treachery; the hurt of having lost him had at last outweighed the joy of having had him, and the sadness of his death had dimmed for me the happiness of his life. It was now that dimly, with little as yet of real understanding, I began to sense that one might perhaps make a friend of grief; not so much lose it as use it and thus transform it. "In that case" (the echo of an eager young voice came back to me) "in that case, don't you see, it's always possible for a man to transcend himself?"

But transcending oneself can never be an easy task. If this was what I had to do it was clear that I must look outside myself for help, for when I looked within myself I seemed to find, just now, chiefly a great confusion.

Then (for after all, I had been raised within the Church) I remembered a certain promise: "Seek and ye shall find; knock and it shall be opened unto you."

I had never tried the promise. I was not at all certain that it would work. I was sure of one thing only; that now at last I was passionately committed to the quest, that I meant to seek and to knock and to discover whether thereby I found, whether thereby a door opened.

11

It was now that I began to read everything I could find that dealt, or that I hoped might deal, with the problem of adjustment to death. "Are you finding what you want?" my husband asked gently one evening, watching me propped up in bed, books strewn about me, taking notes.

I looked at him a bit helplessly. I didn't know—yet. And he sighed, just a little.

"Does it worry you—my trying to find it?" I asked.

He shook his head. "No, of course not. It's only—seeing you going at it with such intensity—night after night . . ." His eyes were pitying. "It isn't really that hard," he said. "It is for me," I told him bleakly. "Exactly that hard."

The objective of my quest was not crystal clear to me of course. I wanted to know what good minds had thought about humanity's great problem, and whether Christians actually could and did reconcile death with something loving and kind at the heart of the universe. I wanted, through reading others, to find out what, if anything, I myself truly believed. I wanted to decide how much of that one lovely experience I had had I might safely keep. And more simply I wanted to find a better way of meeting grief than I had yet discovered.

What I did not want was just to muddle through until time had formed a protective scab. I had by now become aware that time did form such a scab, given enough of it. Like nearly everyone else who has lost someone deeply loved and vividly joyous, someone whose going leaves life not alone sadder, but duller, I rebelled against this idea. All the same, I was beginning to know that it was true. One might lie on his bed and wail for days, if he were so inclined, but sooner or later, if he was not going to die himself (and it happens very, very seldom for a reason like this) he would have to get up, wash his face, smooth his hair and eat a meal. Short of retiring to a monastery (perhaps even there, for all I know) life claimed you relentlessly, dragged you back.

But what I wanted was something a little different. I did not want to lose anything of my child; I wanted to remember everything, keep everything he had given me, and yet learn to live fully and contentedly in a present where he was not. I wasn't sure this combination was possible but it was the only solution that could really satisfy me, the only one that would not leave a hard, unresolved core of bitterness.

It seems strange, even to me now, that I did not as yet in my reading turn to the Bible, the traditional source of comfort and assurance. But I shrank oddly from doing so. I had the feeling that at this stage I would not find help there; knowing, without putting it into words, that a certain block existed at that point within me.

Perhaps the Biblical words were too familiar to me; their very accustomedness may have hid their meaning from me and dulled the terrific impact they have so many times had on those who have read them for the first time. Perhaps I felt irrationally that the Bible had had its chance with me—hadn't I practically been raised on it?—and that it hadn't seemed to help when I most needed help. At any rate there certainly was, in spite of the further inconsistent fact that I was deeply loyal to my Church and to the ideals of Christianity, a definite hindrance that kept me from seeking the Bible just now.

Since both my parents had been kindly, tolerant people on

friendly and loving terms with their Lord, I certainly could not have derived any idea of a stern Deity from them. Indeed, I do not think that my idea was so much of a stern Deity as of one whom I can only characterize by the ridiculous adjective "smug"—and I have no idea from whence I derived it. Perhaps from some forgotten Sunday School teacher, or some preacher heard long ago and equally forgotten. At any rate, I built up a picture when I was somewhat too young to be wholly responsible for it all by myself, of God as someone pompous and patronizing, speaking in unctuous, rolling periods, pretending to be very loving but actually pouncing on one's least misdeed and thereafter piously "forgiving" one.

If it sounds feeble-minded (I admit it does), it wasn't conscious, of course, or formulated. If it had been, surely it could not have survived, for it was a picture so idiotic that the slightest breath of reason must have dispelled it. Whatever the Creator of all beauty, all joy, all life, is, He could not possibly be an absurd old gentleman! Nor would I have admitted, at any period of my grown-up life that I had such a picture. Nevertheless, it lingered. I had discarded it in the same way that my brother had discarded his five-year-old idea, conceived from fascinatedly watching the headgear of a certain lady in the choir on Sundays, that God wore a hat festooned with gold lace. Naturally at thirty-five he no longer actually believed that God was draped with gold lace; nevertheless he was just that age when he admitted to me somewhat ruefully that he still *saw* Him like that.

So, in these early explorations, I read nearly everything *but* the Bible.

For a while it seemed to me that comparatively little had been written which bore with any directness on the enlightenment I wanted first; enlightenment as to what others had thought and felt about death. This surprised me. Because now that I was myself awake to it, it appeared to me a psychological adjustment of such major importance in anybody's life, that I could not understand why there wasn't a vast library about it available. Even the psychological and "self-help" books themselves largely ignored it. I wondered discouragedly if the reason was that nobody had an answer.

As a matter of fact, it seemed to me that most of the "self-help" books proceeded on the same cheerful assumption I myself had for so long enjoyed—that death was too remote and unlikely to be any concern of the average individual's and that to consider it at all, outside of providing insurance for one's family, was on the whole pretty morbid. So if they did deal with it, it was usually in a kind of hurried and in-passing attitude—a mere paragraph or two—as if at some point the author had suddenly said to himself:

"Hold on! I've got to include something for people in sorrow, people who've lost someone important in their lives. And then there are the hopelessly ill ones and the quite old ones—folks facing death for themselves soon. What shall I say to *them?*"

What he thereupon included for the first group (I usually had the feeling, here, that an odd embarrassment seeped through the pages, as if the writer knew that he was discussing a subject that was taboo as "morbid") seemed to me to come to about this: that grief was, of course, inevitable in time of loss, and must run its course like an illness, but time would cure the illness, and anyway, when there was nothing in the world to be done about a thing, you might as well stop thinking about it—also that you must always bear in mind that life was more important than death (with the plain implication that you, as one of the fortunate and superior beings still alive, were more important than anyone for whom you grieved) and therefore as life moved forward, death must be left behind.

However much practical truth this contained, from my point of view it was inadequate. Partly because, as I have said, healing through forgetting was not what I wanted— nor was healing through mere dulling what I wanted, either; and partly because of the obvious fact that, in reality, as life moved forward, death never was left behind; that all life moved forward to, actually, *was* death . . . and that I didn't intend to trick myself into ignoring this again.

As for the second group—the ill, the aged—what the self-help author had for them seemed to boil down to the brisk advice not to give up hope yet (this along with some stories about people who'd been given up by doctors but had nevertheless lived to incredible old ages) because healing powers could yet be set in motion by constructive, healthful thinking, and there was no telling how long they might still be around.

I didn't wholly disagree with this solution, either; I was willing to concede that there might be life in the old dog yet—and I heartily approve of constructive thinking. I simply felt again that it dodged the essential point; since all the healthful thinking in the world wasn't going to do anything but postpone the moment which must finally be met.

I ran across several authors who suggested, sometimes in quite beautiful and poetic language, that our *true* immortality, the only one for which we ought to ask, was to be found in the perpetuation of our "influence" in the lives of others. Sometimes I think I must be hampered by too literal a mind. To me that was one of those statements that sound very fine, have a really noble ring, and simply don't mean anything. Because influence is one thing and immortality is quite another; and to say that the one *is* the other doesn't convince me. I, for instance, feel a warm happiness that Goodrich's life does still deeply influence a good many people yet living; but it is *I* who feel it. He, if he is completely dead, certainly does not. So how does that contribute to his personal immortality? Besides, one runs up against the same old blank wall; since all the people one "influences" must also die, the end is still no more or less than a pile of ashes.

Perhaps the writers who puzzled me most were half a dozen or more whom I knew to be of intellectual caliber far superior to my own who took two positions, both closely related, which my own lesser intelligence was forced to reject. One of these was to the effect that if man would only develop his capacities to their fullest extent here on earth, it would become unimportant to him whether there were a future life or not; the other, the thesis that men in this modern age had lost interest in the idea of a life after death and honestly just did not care.

I tried my best to understand this and failed. It did not seem possible to me that any normal person, not surrendered to a counsel of despair, any vigorous person who loved living, could truly not care about his own survival. It did not seem possible to me that he could contemplate the death of one dear to him and say, "It doesn't matter to me in the least whether he's alive or dead—I'm not interested in whether he goes on or simply stops." I wondered if these writers were somewhat as I myself used to be—individuals who had not yet suffered losses that had struck them at vital points and who had managed airily to persuade themselves that the whole matter was too remote to concern them. But no; some of these men could not be accused of that sort of fantasy. So I could only speculate at last that perhaps they had taken an attitude born of disbelief; since they felt sincerely that there was no future, it was easier to also suppose they didn't much care, anyway. . . . But that any normal human being actually did not, I found I simply could not credit.

144

I seized eagerly religious books whose titles indicated that they dealt broadly with the Christian life; for surely, I thought, these writers would treat death as something purposeful rather than destructive. I recall today with a slightly rueful amusement the baffled sensation with which I put a good many of them down. "It seems to me more likely than otherwise," wrote Dean W. L. Sperry in *What We Mean By Religion*, "that there is some permanent part and place in the totality of things for what we know as human thought, with all the affections and the purposes which it embraces." A few pages further I read, "In our moments of perplexity and distress we say, 'Lord to whom shall we go, Thou hast the words of eternal life.' We may be right, we may be wrong; this is our faith."

I may add that I have recently reread Dean Sperry's admirable book with pleasure and profit. At the time it was pushed, along with others that seemed to me to speak in a weak and uncertain voice, to the back of my bookshelves. ("More likely than otherwise" . . . "We may be right, we may be wrong.") I know now that they were not weak and uncertain; they were merely dealing with a point of theology in a cautious and scholarly manner. Not so did Jesus or St. Paul deal with it; but that is another matter and another approach.

Besides I must admit that as I read, it was never, at this stage, in any mood of simple acceptance myself, nor even of complete open-mindedness, so that if I was disappointed at the cautious utterances, still I did not really wholeheartedly accept the ringing affirmations. For I was desperately afraid of taking anything merely because I would have found it comforting to do so, and I was constantly attempting to subject all I read to an overcritical and searching scrutiny.

I suppose it is true to say that basically I was still looking for, hoping to find, the happy ending. But I think it is also true, and fair, to add that the spirit in which I looked was quite different. I was not now attempting to invent one, at any rate. If I had been running away from reality before, I was sincerely trying to find it now. The happy ending—if it existed at all—was certainly, I knew now, not at all like my lost land of illusion. But even while realizing this, I began to discover that I was literally unable to uproot from my heart a stubborn conviction that there must be a happy ending, eventually. Else the whole business was really "sound and fury, signifying nothing," and life itself a sort of cruel indignity to put upon a being with so much inherent nobility as Man. But that it *was* sound and fury, that life *was* an indignity—this, I was not merely temperamentally in revolt against, I was unable to convince myself that it was a reasonable belief.

For if death were an enemy—again and again in my slow and painful thinking I kept returning to this same place—then so was life an enemy. Since life and death were indivisible, since they could not possibly be separated, since they were both a part of the same process, you could not, no you could *not*, classify the one as good, the other as bad. If half the apple was rotten, it was a bad apple, and don't be deceived by the fact that the first few bites tasted delicious and seemed juicy and firm. A few more, and you'd find on your tongue the bitter flavor of worms and corruption. Then you'd feel quite justified in saying of the whole, "This apple is bad."

I could find no escape from the logic of this conclusion. But the stubborn conviction remained, and as I read it deepened, grew, crystallized; I could not believe that life was bad. Persistently, no matter in what blind alleys I found myself wandering, I kept on feeling that life was a gift of very great value; that even when it was hard, it still was valuable; that it was, in fact, highly important to get born.

It was now that I began to wonder whether my happy ending might not turn out to be, after all, no ending but a new, and better, beginning.

And if this intuition was a true one, if indeed death was not bad, being an indispensable part of something good and an entrance into something better, then there must be some method by which intelligence would come into harmony with it. In spite of pain, in spite of loss, come, literally, into harmony with it.

I was dim as to what coming into harmony with death involved; but I was clear on one point—that all other solutions, however brave and good, in essence merely made the best of a bad matter. Which, in turn, completed the circle and brought me right back where I'd started; to the reiterated point that if death was a bad matter, then so was life, and that this last I did not, could not, believe.

12

At first, as I have indicated, I had undertaken this faltering research of mine into another realm of thought hesitatingly, even with a certain tension and anxiety, and often a sense of futility. Then one day—it seemed to happen rather suddenly without my quite knowing how, or when—I realized that this was gone and in its place had grown up an eagerness. More, a sort of stir of my blood as if I were approaching something not clearly seen but tremendously vital and exciting in its dimly glimpsed outlines. It was almost as if some sixth sense were saying, while I pressed deeper into a new landscape, "You're getting closer!" Perhaps a bird flying south for the first time, a bird who had never felt the softness of the southern air or caught the scent of southern fragrances, might nevertheless know in somewhat that same fashion, by the pulsing of its being, that it was nearing a place unfamiliar, unimagined, yet somehow mysteriously and uniquely its destiny.

I had begun a journey that was to lead me, at last, straight to those I had thought were "lost"; that was to make my son, my brother, my parents, once more an active part of my daily life. Nor must I forget that it was to much more than relief from the heavy burden of grief that it led; it led to a vastly deepened sense, as well, of the importance of life. Life in every phase, this one and the future one. And it led also to a serenity no longer entirely dependent on circumstance; and along with a richer happiness in living here and now, no more fear of dying, absolutely none, rather an eager sense of a great experience ahead.

Let me hurry to add that I am not saying that all this happened quickly or that it followed any regular pattern; nor that I did not many times in good old Methodist fashion (it happens that I *am* a Methodist) fall from grace. And Heaven forbid that I should seem even to hint that the process is anywhere near complete. On the contrary, I must be constantly striving not just to attain deeper insight and grow more, but also merely to maintain what I have. Unless I reaffirm my position almost every day, unless I go back every day to the source of my help, I find myself backsliding (another good Methodist word) again. Nevertheless it is true that at about this time a new Earth, and a new Heaven, began to open before me, and that the vision has never since wholly deserted me.

I did not then know quite what was happening to me. I do not now, in any literal sense. What I do know is that the magic of that promise "Knock and it shall be opened" was beginning to work for me. For it is a magic promise. I do not understand; probably I cannot understand; but I am utterly certain that genuine, sustained knocking—searching—asking (by which, of course, I do not mean shouting hysterically at God)—does actually set in motion forces which respond almost magnetically to the sincerity and the urgency of that effort. It is true that I was reaching rather blindly, in helter-skelter fashion; and I had not even learned yet to go to the Source itself. Nevertheless I was reaching; earnestly, sincerely, constantly. So, in a measure, I was receiving; so, a little way, the door was opening.

Reading what other people had thought and felt about life and death and God was, for me, a natural way of seeking to discover what I myself could believe. I had always read a great deal. I had been the sort of child of whom her elders complain, "Her nose is always in a book!" But my reading had been mostly fiction, and at first, as I have indicated, I stumbled through this different sort of literature with dissatisfaction and even at times with rebellion. Then, under my husband's guidance, I began to find those confident, ringing assertions of faith in an unseen power which have come down to us from many great men through the ages; and to find, too, that they woke in me something that had been sleeping. There was a dignity, a majesty, a profundity and a deep serenity about the best of them that thrilled me like great music, giving me that same strange, almost mystic tingle. Like great music also I did not quite understand, but the sound was inexpressibly stirring.

I found the other assertions, too, of course; the assertions of the disciples of Purposelessness, those who apparently sincerely believed that everything had happened by accident, that there was no order, no design, no purpose in the Universe; no God; and no life for man but this one. There was nobility of a grim sort in many of these, too. They sometimes spoke, it seemed to me, with an almost agonized sincerity; and they faced their terrible blank wall with courage.

But, increasingly, as I acquired a background against which my own steadily growing beliefs could take shape, I found that these men puzzled me. They argued with such passion for their dreary theories, they were so intensely purposeful themselves in their eagerness to find explanations and their insistence on preserving their intellectual integrity —how did they account for themselves, I wondered? How had they, and others like them, arrived on the scene at all in this accidental coalition of things?

In large measure they seemed to me to be refuting their

own arguments even while they argued; refuting them just by being the kind of people they were. For though they talked of purposelessness, the terms they used were purposeful; and most of them were insistent that still it was better to be kind than cruel, better to be unselfish than selfish, in short, better to be good than bad. But goodness, I thought, is a highly positive and purposeful trait, so weren't they using words that they themselves had robbed of meaning?

Religion appeared to most of them, I gathered, to be at best a delusion and at worst an opiate to soothe people who didn't have the honesty or courage to face "reality." But they had a religion themselves, of a dark sort—the religion of no-religion; and they preached it as zealously as any missionary. I actually came across a statement by one prominent philosopher that in the acceptance of this no-purpose, no-God, all-accident theory lay the only road to "salvation" . . . a remark which sent me into a brown study. Salvation for *whom*? Surely not for poor old mankind—whose brief stay here is pretty often uncomfortable and whose speedy end is annihilation.

Finally it became clear to me (and I found it rather comforting) that no matter what dark theory a man evolved, he went right on—as long as he was sane—behaving like a purposeful creature. He might think the universe was an accident but he continued to plan his own life and to build for the lives of his children. He acted like this for the best of reasons; that was the kind of being he was, and he couldn't help doing it. Which, again, brought me right back to the point from which I'd started; that it was hard to believe that purpose had got here by accident.

It is not, however, my intention to rehearse arguments as I speak of these two great streams of thought of which I became aware; these two currents which have flowed down to us through the centuries from Plato and earlier, which one author has described as the affirming and the denying stream. Much has been written on both sides and all is available to interested readers. So I need only say here that to me, slowly but with increasing surety, it began to seem that the voices which spoke for affirmation were not only nobler but more rational; that the intelligences from which they proceeded were at once loftier and more penetrating; above all, perhaps, that they were based on some type of strangely vital experience which gave them a living, glowing, vibrant quality that made the others seem unreal by comparison, poor and thin, sterile and lifeless.

I realized that neither side could "prove" its points, in the laboratory meaning of that word "proof." But this one thing seemed to me to be utterly true; that no matter what theory one held about how man and the universe came into being, one was forced at last in any sort of reconstruction, whether it be labeled mechanistic or religious, to arrive at the Thing that had no beginning, the Thing that always was. For if this was an intensely mysterious idea from which reason shied away, yet it was also an idea to which reason itself reluctantly forced one back. You could not forever keep saying, "Before this, was that; and that, in turn, evolved from the other; and the other sprang from something else; and behind the something else . . ." No, that soon became impossible. And finally even the most "materialistic" mind was forced to the conclusion, "There has to be something that never was created, that always existed."

For myself, when I reached this point, I found it entirely impossible to accept the notion that this Eternal Something could be Matter, or Energy, or any mindless force whatsoever, called by any name. I discovered that while I could not understand God, I could conceive Him; but this other —this mindless force which had somehow by sheer chance evolved the astronomer's beautifully mathematical universe —was inconceivable. And it became more so when I tried to go a step further and to add that in its mechanistic mindlessness this force had also produced beings who could think and plan and love, and that from its impersonal machinery had sprung the wonder of personality.

At any rate, I could not help feeling that the only thing the "denier" escaped, in his revolt against religious faith and religious intuition, was the necessity for believing in a Creator. For in the final analysis his five senses could no more demonstrate eternal, creative Matter—or Energy or any other like force—than they could demonstrate God. Therefore his mechanistic philosophy required, it seemed to me, quite as much "faith" and quite as much "intuition" as the religious explanation. It also struck me as being fully as "mystic" and definitely even more mysterious.

The agnostic, of course, had another answer. "I quite agree. All you're saying is that neither one of you can *know*. That's my theory, too. I don't know and I know that I don't know."

But going back again to the great "affirmations" I felt suddenly and deeply that these men did know; they knew in the way even the most ordinary, unspeculative individual knows the greatest realities of his life which, nevertheless, he cannot, could not, prove—through experience and feeling; as he knows that he loves his wife and his children, as he knows that certain intangibles like honesty and kindness matter more than any of the tangibles, as he knows that when he is in trouble, prayer "helps."

Lecomte du Noüy, in his well-known *Human Destiny* opens his first chapter with these sentences: "Two different paths may eventually lead to the comprehension of man. The first, revelation, is a direct road, but is closed to a great many people and independent of rational thought. Those who can make use of it are fortunate. The second, on the contrary, is strictly rational and scientific."

I shall not argue the question as to whether Mr. du Noüy is altogether right in separating these two "paths" so sharply; as to whether they do not, indeed, often converge, and whether, in any event, both are not finally necessary to that "comprehension of man." Nor shall I do more than

156

state in passing my own conviction that the direct way is not closed to any averagely intelligent and rational person who will open himself to it. What is significant is that a great scientist thus recognizes the place of direct intuition. And this is a trend in science with which we are now becoming more and more familiar.

Call it by any name you like—intuition, constructive imagination, perception—man does have another sense besides the five we can catalogue, an increasing number of scientists are declaring; a sense which puts him in touch with that core of himself which he deeply feels to be unphysical and also with something else he as deeply feels to be outside himself and bigger than he. This sense is a part of his heritage, and without it he would be a dull clod.

Einstein talks of the same sense in a small book called *Cosmic Religion*. It is greater, he says, than knowledge which is bounded by the five senses; and he adds that it is mainly responsible for his own greatest scientific discoveries and, in his opinion, for all the truly great scientific discoveries ever made. (I fancy Mr. Einstein would readily admit that this intuition must be grounded in knowledge.) Probably not even the most confirmed "materialist" has ever doubted that it is responsible for great artistic achievements. (Which also need knowledge and training as foundation.) And the two realms which we have, perhaps mistakenly, thought of as so sharply separated seem to merge into one with the remarkable statement by a prominent scientist who worked at Oak Ridge, that the cracking of the atom was as much a spiritual and artistic achievement as a scientific one; and that often when it seemed that they were being most daring in their intuitive, imaginative leaps out into space, it turned out that they were right.

It was this sense which I did not fully perceive, while he was living, in the boy who went down in the Baltic; but which shines now so bright and clear to the view of all of us who loved him.

He had left behind him, when he flew overseas, a volume of Plato, heavily marked. (He had majored in Philosophy while in college.)

"I don't understand why a person like you doesn't read Plato," he said, arranging his books on the shelves while I stood by. "Honestly, Mother, you should."

So now I read Plato, having tried to prepare myself a little beforehand by reading the first textbook which he'd studied in his initial course in Philosophy. Even with this background, I cannot possibly claim that I understood anywhere near all of Plato. But some of those lofty and beautiful concepts did emerge for me, and in any event, even when I did not understand, I think Plato was partly responsible for the wonderful thing that now began to happen to me. It is a thing very difficult to put into words. Perhaps the simplest way to express it is just to say that the world of the unseen which all my life had been near me as a sort of fairyland into which I deliberately escaped at will, never for an instant endowing it with any attribute of actuality, slowly took shape and, in changed form, assumed the aspects of reality.

My horizons were pushed out almost startlingly and a certain sense of eager adventure was born, as if life and the world had suddenly become immensely more interesting and exciting.

It is difficult to express sheer sensation in words. But think back to that lovely anticipation you felt when very young, that touching certainty that someday something wonderful was sure to happen to you. You probably never visualized fully just what it was going to be, but you knew it would be thrilling and glorious and above all different from the ordinary, commonplace lives of your elders. And any day it might happen; the next closed door you opened might lead you straight to it, it might be hidden just around the next corner waiting for you.

Ah well, most of us have felt this—and practically all of us lose it as we grow older. I doubt if it persists even into the late twenties, for the average person. Most of us have discovered by then that even if life is full and rich and utterly rewarding, nothing of the magical sort we dreamed of is going to come to us. Perhaps what does come may be better. And indeed the bright vision dies so slowly and its going is so natural a development that it is practically painless and seldom later recalled, save in brief flashes, and without disappointment.

But for me this new sense of the reality of the unseen and the stirring possibility of penetrating and exploring a little way into its secret gardens, gave back that feeling of breathless anticipation which is youth's especial heritage.

And I realized (again with that tingling sense of drawing near something immensely big and important) how far the wholehearted acceptance of what we have called the affirmative position, plus this vital emotional awareness of an unseen world, could go toward relieving some of humanity's most gruesome fears. The fear of death must change character then, must greatly diminish; the worst blackness of grief must lighten. There would be left, for oneself, the natural, proper, healthy effort of the physical organism to continue living as long as possible and the reluctance to leave loved people and pursuits and surroundings; and there would be left, in the loss of loved individuals, the pain of absence. But neither of these is at all like the shrinking horror the soul feels at facing extinction, or the grinding heartbreak of the conviction that one very dear has ceased to be, just is not any more, anywhere.

Surely, too, I thought, the fear and sadness of seeing old age approach (which to some people is worse than the fear of death) must grow less. Because the failing of one's powers, the relinquishment of activity, is only a part of that sadness and would not be unbearable if one were sure it was only temporary and something intensely interesting and vital still were ahead. The other part, the part that hurts most, is the sense of things ending, the dreary conviction that one's future is gone, and that the rest of the short way is all downhill with the happiest things forever behind.

But suppose the most thrilling adventure of all were ahead —for oneself and all those one loved! And suppose one really believed this—not just held it as a pallid theological dogma, but truly believed it with one's heart and blood and mind, counted on it as one counts on the fact that tomorrow is coming!

Was it this that Thomas Wolfe was thinking and feeling when he wrote, "Something has spoken to me in the night, burning the tapers of the waning year . . . to lose the earth you know, for greater knowing; to lose the life you have, for greater life; to leave the friends you love for greater loving . . . . a wind is rising and the rivers flow."

Greater knowing, greater life, greater loving . . . could this realization be what coming into harmony with death meant?

And now dimly, dimly, but with an indescribable thrill I began to understand a little of what Plato had meant when he talked of the reality beyond the appearance; began to catch—behind the shapes of things as they had always looked to me—a come-and-go but ineffable glimpse of what might just possibly be the lovely shapes of things as they were. And along with these half-discerned glimpses came a fresh, poignant realization about the boy who was gone.

(But was he? Sometimes, lately, he seemed so near.)

For looking back, remembering so much that he had said and written, remembering his shining-eyed radiance before beauty of sight or sound, I saw that this sense of a beauty beyond the appearance, transcending it but gleaming through it, had been intensely present to him, whether he had ever consciously formulated it or not. What else could he have been feeling when he said that he never listened to great music without the keen awareness that it stemmed from a much bigger power than the man who was playing it, and even bigger than the man who had composed it? What else when he talked of that spiritual glow, that glimpse into infinite beauty that came as he listened to a great pianist? And oh, what else, when, in faltering, boyish way he tried to tell us—as a child sleeping on the mountaintop, as a young man flying in the sky and looking down on the Pilot's Cross—how a door had swung part way open, and he had barely glimpsed glory beyond?

I had not known what he had been struggling to express then. I had been only vaguely proud without understanding. But now, suddenly and joyously, I was able to share with him, a little at least, that exultant moment when he'd felt as if he'd known, dimly (he said), what "the whole darn business was about"—and that dying was a very great adventure.

With that I felt again, as actual as if a warm, strong wind had blown on me, the lovely sensation I had known once before; the sensation of his pleasure. As if he laughed aloud; as if he cried, "At last!"

"It is not," writes John Baillie, famous Scottish preacher and theologian, "that by some great effort I can attain belief; but that by no effort, however great, can I avoid it."

How hard men tried to avoid it, I thought wonderingly! How they argued and turned and twisted and doubled on their tracks to avoid it! And how inevitably, sooner or later, in one way or another, at one time of crisis or another, they betrayed the fact that they found it impossible to avoid it.

So now in genuine searching, in genuine humility for my stupidly closed mind, I did turn back to the Bible. And there, in the greatest, the noblest, the most majestically ringing affirmations of all, I found—feeling again, as I read, that mysterious thrill as of mighty music—the eternal substance of that which all the affirmers had been saying down through the ages.

13

I suppose there is no one, from the great saints on down to the ordinary, stumbling human beings like myself, who has not had to learn that beautiful visions fade and seem to the disappointed gaze of the seeker, for discouraging intervals, to be lost entirely; that widened horizons shrink and narrow dismayingly and the former splendid distances are shut off by fog and mist; that the lovely light which seemed for a time to permeate even the most commonplace, drab, familiar objects, touching them with magic, has become once more, by some sad alchemy, only the unrevealing daylight one has known before.

Or is it unrevealing, one is tempted to wonder despondently? Maybe *this* is the reality. Maybe it was the other that was illusion.

It is not true. Deep in one's heart, one knows it is not true. For there is about an authentic spiritual vision, an authentic spiritual contact, a vividness that dwarfs material reality. One knows with an unassailable knowledge that reaches into heart and blood and bones and spirit that one has had a glimpse of something that is permanent, indestructible and splendid.

All the more, then, its apparent leaving comes as a shock and a bitter disappointment. And each time as one emerges from such a "lost" period and the Unseen begins again to inform the Seen with new life and color—each time one thinks:

Now, surely, at last, I have it for keeps and for good!

And each time, for me at any rate, it goes again and once more I seem completely earthbound.

It took me quite a long time to realize that experience in this area only follows the familiar pattern of experience in all other areas. In any field of vision or endeavor we have these "slumps." Almost inexplicably, it seems, we suddenly feel depressed and discouraged and helpless before problems that yesterday we tackled blithely. The happy enthusiasm we felt only a little while ago, and the sense of excited opportunity—where has it all gone? Today we wonder why on earth we ever thought we could do a certain job, why on earth we ever imagined we had certain capabilities.

"Something," said a friend of mine disconsolately, "something inside me seems actually to oppose every worthwhile effort I make! To keep telling me that it's no use and I'll fail anyway. Something seems to *want* me to fail. What in the world can it be?"

I suppose the answer is that it's herself. Psychologists assure us that there is a will to fail as well as a will to succeed, reminding us that failure takes far less effort, demands far less of us, excuses us from much stress. Whatever it may be we have all known this nagging devil within who, as my friend said, "opposes" us. Often, too, our spiritual malaise is the reflection of some subconscious conflict or some worry we have not acknowledged; and it may also be due to a physical maladjustment. In short—there can be a hundred causes. Maybe they all boil down to the fact that we're human.

But even aside from what one writer has quaintly called "the drag of the flesh," there is something else that I failed for quite a while to realize as a factor in these disconcerting losses of spiritual awareness; which is that a vision is practically never synonomous with an achievement. Long ago I had learned—again in other areas—that no desirable condition, no desirable accomplishment, was possible for me without genuine and sustained effort. Whatever I wanted that was very much worth having I had to work not only to get but to maintain. And this was as true of intangibles as of tangibles; as true of attitudes and qualities I desired— kindness, friendliness, good temper, patience, integrity— and of conditions I wished to promote—a harmonious home life, a happy marriage—as it was of the automobile I had to economize first to buy and afterward to keep running.

I would have saved myself a good many hours of discouragement if I had seen this sooner; if I had realized that the necessity for self-discipline and the courage to persist apply as much, and even more, to the achievement of spiritual contact and awareness as they do to any other achievement.

This, of course, is actually only very plain common sense. The musician cannot give up practising on the days when he does not feel inclined toward the piano and his performance seems heavy and dull. He has to practise good days and bad. The writer who finally finishes anything worth reading spends many hours on what appears to be quite unproductive labor, typing page after page that he stuffs into the wastebasket. The point is that hours like this aren't really unproductive at all. They are a necessary and inevitable element of the whole creative process, and there is a sense in which the dull practise hours, the "wasted" pages, are as much a part of the finished product as the successful hours, the pages that are kept. It simply means what we all know—what is the most commonplace and familiar of truths—that interest and zest and inspiration desert everyone at times; and that if the individual despairs whenever that happens and sits numbly to wait for them to come back, the condition is extremely likely to become permanent.

Personally, I have learned now to be philosophical about these spiritual slumps. I know they are going to recur; I'm only happy to note that they come less often and last less long. And I know, too, how I must behave when they do come. I must repel and refuse discouragement with all my might, for that is a numbing, deadening thing which saps vitality. I must learn to say—and to believe—"I'll get past this dull stretch" (or maybe even "this bad stretch") "if I hold fast to faith and effort." I must keep on steadily, even when I feel an actual distaste (which is half sheer indolence) for doing so, with the practices and the gestures which I have found from experience will help bring back what I seem to have lost; praying, reading the words and talking with the people that inspire, consciously reaching for contact with the spiritual world, making a strong, imaginative effort toward spiritual awareness, maintaining a constant faith in what I believe is true even when I can no longer feel it to be true.

It is valuable, if one can, to find out why the slump and the dullness came; and sometimes it is possible. Honest examination will frequently discover some transgression against the laws of health, or some deep dissatisfaction with one's own attitudes and behavior, or some nagging, unadmitted worry. But whether one finds the cause or whether it remains just one of those mysterious ebbs of the human spirit, the way back is the same; the courage to hold fast to faith and to endeavor.

At last I began to see that just as the "wasted" pages were not truly wasted, so the sterile times might be times of strange growth, if only I could summon the character not to yield to discouragement and weariness, to disillusionment and a sense of futility.

My hidden fear of death was so old and so deep, my immediate background of grief was so poignant, that to alter emotional attitudes which had "set" to this extent was—and is—a job which must be done again and again. I think it surprised me somewhat, at first, to find that this was true. In the first lovely flush of relief at the emotional conviction that my parents, my brother, my son still lived, I did not take this into account. Also there was something else I had not realized: besides the enemies within oneself, there are certain outside influences to be combatted if one is to attain this different feeling about the fact of death.

For it is hard to push against a strong current of general opinion and emotion; and there is no doubt that a very large part of humanity, even Christian humanity, regards death with terror and hatred. Of course it is easy to see that there is a sense in which this feeling is natural and necessary. Every normal living organism fights hard to live; otherwise life on this planet would have perished almost simultaneously with its beginning. So if one believes that

God has a plan for this world; that ready-made angels did not, somehow, fit into that plan; that this first phase of life had to be (we cannot know why) a physical one; then it follows that a passionate will to survive, physically, was vitally essential to the Plan.

I felt this to be true so deeply that occasionally I found myself wondering, in some confusion, if the people who had little of this will to live now (one meets them sometimes) were not so lacking in some vital, essential spark, that there might not have to be a long period of re-education under better conditions, before they would much like living in the next phase of life, either. "Poor Carlyle," Leigh Hunt is supposed to have remarked, at Carlyle's death. "He won't like God."

Nevertheless, it also seemed to me that a Christian, two thousand years after Jesus had promised many mansions and Paul had pictured that glorious body celestial, should be able to express this vital law of survival quite normally in his own behavior—even realizing that any other course was wrong and hostile to that great Plan—and yet transcend the horrified aversion to death. Surely, at any rate, I thought, as we grew older the prospect ought to begin to seem sweeter, more natural; even tinged with gaiety and a sense of adventure. And I could not see that this happened at all frequently.

I realized that one must not confuse the fear of death with the shrinking from the act of dying, of course. The latter still seems to me as natural as the shrinking one feels from any physical ordeal—from having a tooth pulled to undergoing an operation. But nurses and doctors insist almost universally that the fear of dying is usually ungrounded; that nature is most often kind at the end. And in any event this is the kind of fear with which we are accustomed to deal, which surely by maturity we should have learned to handle. The fear of being dead is a different matter; and I began finally to feel that something must be terribly awry with our picture of life after death.

I have said, earlier, that one of the most painful aspects of grief is a certain dreadful pity the living are prone to feel for the dead. Even after my younger son had shown me so clearly, on that ride to New York, how irrational this feeling was, I continued to find it hard to shake off. So at last it occurred to me that perhaps this was partly, at any rate, because I met the idea at every turn; because nearly everybody else seemed to feel that way, too. "Poor John"— "Poor Mary"—they said of the dead. I remember vividly the sudden stab I felt one morning when, conning the newspaper over a pleasant, leisurely breakfast, I turned to my favorite columnist, and discovered that he was writing that day about the overseas graves of boys killed in battle, and that he had headed his column with a phrase from a poem —"The Lonely Dead." I sat there, my food turned to ashes in my mouth, tears stinging behind my lids, seeing only a white cross with *his* name on it an ocean away, feeling only the desolation and the bitterness of those words applied to *him*—"the lonely dead."

And I found then that, curiously enough, my mind had gone back to some childhood pictures; I took my reading, in those days, in cycles—certain eras, certain authors, occupying me exclusively for one particular phase before I moved on to another—and somewhere between eight and ten I reached the Greek mythology stage and read that and nothing else for months. I played dramatic games about the heroes and gods and goddesses of those immortal stories, and I remember very well Edwin's indignation at being assigned the role of Hector while I took Achilles—I had painstakingly explained to him that "Hector was the nicest"—when he discovered that Hector in the end got dragged three times around the wall of Troy. Now, with the memory of that time suddenly close and clear, I knew that along with a taste for great literature and (doubtless) many high concepts, I had got something else from those tales; a very dismal picture of the nature of life after physical death. The idea that I had been left with (nor am I saying that this was what all the Greeks believed nor that one doesn't find the same idea in the legends of many other nations) was that a favored few, very few, when they died were destined for the Elysian Fields; but that the majority became "ghosts," pallid shades who wandered desolately in an unspeakably dreary half-world, always looking back with wistful yearning to the light and the warmth they had forever left, always "hovering"—as my kindly acquaintance's grandmother had thought—on the outskirts of "real" life, bystanders only, never again participants.

I think there is no arguing with the fact that this picture is—probably as a rule quite unconsciously—exceedingly widespread, wherever it came from. I almost guarantee that anyone who begins to watch for it, in what he reads and what he hears, can pile up a dozen instances in as many days with no difficulty at all.

Not long ago a friend of mine talked to me in distress about a relative whose daughter had been killed in a car accident nearly two years before.

"It's so sad to see her grieving her life away," she sighed. "Jane's such a good Christian—such a hard church worker. I think the trouble is that every time she feels a little better, she thinks she's being disloyal to Anne. 'How can I be gay when my child had to *die?*' she moans—and then she's off again."

"But you said she was a Christian," I couldn't help remarking. "In that case—she doesn't believe her child is dead."

"Oh—well—of course. She knows Anne is in Heaven. But we don't have much idea of what that's like, after all."

But to me it seemed that the whole point was not that Jane felt she had no idea of what it was like, but that she had somehow acquired quite definite ideas, and that they were evidently all sad and gruesome. You don't feel disloyal toward one you love because you smile—unless you feel that one is herself lonely and unhappy. In short, Jane had never brought her theological acceptances in line with her emotional ones.

I even discovered these dreary conceptions of existence

173

after death in advertisements. A few years ago a well-known weekly carried a full-page ad showing a transparent wraith ringing the doorbell of an insurance agent. From within the agent and his wife watched, appearing, I must say, quite a lot less startled than one might have supposed they would.

"It can't be Beany," said the caption in huge letters. "Beany's dead!"

Beany it was, nevertheless, returned—of course—to find out if it was not still possible to take out more insurance for his family. He had to be told that it was too late and the subsequent moral need not be pointed. But the interesting thing about it all was the idea the writer managed to convey of Beany's present existence. The agent remarks—and very reasonably, I thought:

"But Beany, you're dead!"

To which Beany replies, "Yeah, I know."

The agent's wife then asks him politely how he is, and he answers, still managing to diffuse that impression of pallid listlessness, "Oh, about as well as could be expected." About as well, one gathers as could be expected of anyone who's *dead*. Beany, in fact, "didn't have much to say about his new location. A quiet kind of place, I gathered. Not much doing."

No, not much doing in the grave. Not much doing, either, in a place where formerly live, solid people exist only as misty wraiths, a place where life is lived on a very dim level

174

indeed. In short, a place which anybody with one spark of vitality must regard with intense dislike.

Even into the Christian conception, this odd, distasteful notion of the grave as an "eternal resting place" where the dead "sweetly sleep," and this like notion of a completely devitalized Heaven, has managed to seep. One cannot but sympathize with the little boy who didn't want to be "one of them damn cherubims" (my father's best-loved joke) and the little girl who inquired plaintively, "If I'm very good in Heaven all week, will they let me go down to Hell and play on Saturdays?" One of Goodrich's favorite cartoons, which he clipped from *The New Yorker* and mailed me, represented two musicians sitting on the edge of a cloud and dolefully strumming harps, while one observed to the other, "I certainly miss my grand piano!"

In a mystery novel lately I ran across a significant little phrase. One of the characters was meditating suicide. She was sick of living and would not have hesitated if she had only been sure there was no life after death. "But supposing death wasn't the end? Suppose, when you'd done it, you found you were still alive—sort of?"

A life "sort of"—yes, I thought, that describes pretty aptly the nature of the life a great many of us do, perhaps quite unconsciously, visualize.

It must be unconscious. Because of course if we stop and think even one moment we know what nonsense this is. There is a kind of logic about the position that there is no life at all after death. That case can, at any rate, be argued intelligently. But to believe that there is another, that some essential part of mankind triumphantly survives the death of the body and goes on, and yet to assume that this second, vastly more advanced, vastly more permanent and indestructible phase of living, is less alive, less vigorous, less interesting, than the first, fragile, temporary stage, is a piece of superstitious unreason whose persistence is hard to understand. Hard, at least, for me . . . who, I know as I look back, had that very idea and that very picture. I suppose that the fear of death and the horror which clings 'round the thought of dissolution has somehow cast its sinister aura even over the surviving spirit.

But it's too bad we can't outgrow it. For in that life a thousand doors must be open that now are closed, a thousand vivid, thrilling experiences waiting of which at present we cannot dream. It's too bad not to have the fun of looking forward to them a bit.

Fortunately there are those who know this. One reads the things they have written, and sometimes one meets them and catches the singing note of joyful anticipation in what they say. A few years ago a widely known young minister—the Reverend Peter Marshall—died suddenly. Only a very short time before his death he startled his congregation by demanding of them suddenly one Sunday morning, "Are you afraid to die?" Then he added, "I'm not. I'm looking forward to it. I can hardly wait. *And I'm not nuts.*"

When I first read this, in the editorial column of a weekly

magazine, I found myself asking in a puzzled sort of manner why a man who was young, successful, happily married, with a child and hundreds of friends, should want to die. I wonder how many of his congregation shared this obtuseness. For it *was* obtuse. Peter Marshall spoke only of a journey that he was sure to take someday and he said, "I'm looking forward to it—sometimes I can hardly wait!" It was no expression of despair, no "I-wish-I-were-dead" remark; very much the contrary. I am sure that he did not wish to "escape" from anything, certainly not from life. Rather, it seems to me, he was expressing a love of life so vital, so springing, so eager, that it included in its sense of happy anticipation *all* of life, this phase and the next. He was so ardent for life that he could hardly wait for it to go on unfolding, and he looked forward with intense eagerness to each new step.

And truly it seems to me that this is just a superbly normal and wholesome manifestation of Christianity. The best-balanced, best-adjusted people are nearly always eager for the future, no matter how fully and satisfactorily they are living in the present. Peter Marshall, in his sure faith, only went a step further than most of us are able to do and was eager for his entire future, not alone the limited and uncertain one physical existence could promise him.

Shortly after Goodrich's death had been confirmed by the Government, a friend from out of town was visiting in my home at the same time that a dear relative was with me. My friend was a person at whom I looked with uncomprehending wonder and a dull envy just then. A year and a half earlier her pilot son had been killed, and her sunny serenity puzzled me deeply. She did her best to tell me its source, to explain to me that the boy did not seem "lost" to her, that after the first hard months he was as real and as present to her as her other living children. But the words never got past my eardrums; they barely reached my mind, much less my heart. It is true, however, that there were many things which people wrote or said to me in those first days that seemed to fall on just such closed ears, but came back later to help me more than the speakers will ever know. And it was as my friend, my relative, and I were wiping dishes in the kitchen that evening that something was said which I have never forgotten.

"I don't understand," my relative suddenly burst out, "why God saved just one boy on that ship! I don't understand why He saved Lieutenant—— and let Goodrich die!"

The woman whose son had been killed was silent a moment, her head bent over the plate she was polishing so carefully. Then she raised it and smiled.

"Oh—saved!" she said cheerfully. "But what do you mean by saved? You see, you're thinking of death as being lost —as the worst thing that can possibly happen to anybody. But it could be that God doesn't feel like that about it at all!"

Thinking it over, I'm almost sure He doesn't.

14

One of the stumbling blocks I had to learn to avoid—one over which I continued at intervals to trip for much too long, even after I knew better, and one which never failed, if I yielded to it, to bring back horror, grief, and the old bad attitudes I was trying to outgrow—was the tendency periodically to revert to identifying my son with the physical fragments he had left behind him.

I am sure that this is an emotion practically universal to love bereft. At first it is so natural as to be inescapable, and one even feels it would be a little inhuman to be able to tear one's affection away immediately from the body that once housed a dearly loved individual. It was, after all, the means by which one knew him, one's only way of contact with him. It was *him,* in short. And for a while it still seems to be him.

But of course it isn't. When Edwin died, all in a moment, Jeannot could not bear immediately to part with what was left. The shock had been too stunning, it had happened too quickly; she instructed the undertaker to bring the body back when he had prepared it. So there it lay, on the bed that they had shared together, for twenty-four hours. But just before the funeral, the following afternoon, she said to me restlessly, as we walked in Edwin's lovely garden:

"I want them to come now—I want them to take it away. It's not him, it's not him!" After a moment she added, "Even Bing knew. He knew it sooner than I did."

Bing was their little dog; and all the day he had been hunting for Edwin. He had trotted into his closet and sniffed at his shoes, whining softly; he had padded uneasily from one end of the house to the other. But never once, for the entire twenty-four hours that the waxen image of Edwin lay on that bed, did he approach it or show the faintest interest in what was there. His instinct at this point was true; it was not the Master for Bing.

Of course this does not mean that tenderness will not continue to surround and to hallow the places where the bones our beloveds used have been placed; but then tenderness surrounds and hallows the other things they touched and used, the other things associated with them. It is only when one pours out on a coffin the love which belonged—and belongs—to the living person, that any genuine sense of that vital, living person as he is *now* is inevitably lost.

As for me, I finally came to realize that I simply could not afford to think at all of those coffins. This may not be equally true for everyone. I do know one elderly man who visits his wife's grave each day and I do not think he feels for a moment that her gay spirit is imprisoned there in darkness, or that there is anything "morbid" about his visits. Each one is simply, for him, a rendezvous. He somehow finds it easier to meet her there. But I doubt that most of us would. At any rate, the contrary is true for me; and I realized this forcibly once and for all when the bodies of the soldiers who had met death overseas began to come home.

I will never forget that October afternoon when the first contingent arrived in our own city. THE BOYS COME HOME IN NARROW QUARTERS! the headlines shouted in big letters. The article beneath those headlines was well-written. It was tender and moving. Yet I read it with a mounting dismay. As I finished each sentence I kept hoping that somewhere in the next one there would be a word, a phrase, at least a hint that after all the boys themselves were not in those coffins; that they had moved on elsewhere.

I found no such hint. There was not even the faintest gleam of sunlight through cypress trees. There was nothing to give any hope or comfort to those who were waiting for those caskets. There was everything to break a heart into a hundred shattered bits all over again and drive home ruthlessly the cruel difference between what had sailed away and what was coming home.

My thoughts went back, then, to a day, the summer before, when my husband had brought home some blanks on which we were to designate what we wanted done with our son's body.

"I've had them three weeks," he'd confessed.

It re-opened—distressingly, for me—a subject I had thought was settled. Goodrich was buried in Sweden and the Swedes, in the letters and the pictures they had sent us, in the imposing military funeral they had given the unknown young flyer, had shown a heavenly kindness. All three of us—my husband, Chap, and I—had agreed that we wanted his coffin left where it was.

But now, we were told, it was going to be moved. This was necessary because he was not buried in a permanent American cemetery. The Government's idea was clear; it intended to make sure of permanent care for the grave of every American soldier whose family did not take that responsibility from its shoulders. So it said in effect, "Choose a permanent American cemetery at home or abroad, and we will bury his body there and look after the grave forever. Or tell us in what private cemetery you want him buried, and we will send his coffin there to you."

If we were not going to bring his body home, then the obvious choice was France, as near as possible to the Brittany coast where his beloved French aunt now lived. There would be something sweet and fitting about this—both because of the close bond that had existed between them and because he loved France and once spent an idyllically happy summer there with his brother.

Nevertheless, to me the idea of disinterment was unspeakably painful. So painful that it centered my thoughts constantly on that casket, and brought back the old, wild, horror that what was in it was all that was left of *him*. So morbid did I become that I even began to wonder whether it was not a species of cowardly disloyalty in me not to "bring him home"—as if somehow I had refused and rejected him.

Fortunately at this point common sense intervened with the reminder of what his own attitude had been. Two incidents came back to me, both illustrating that special quality which was his, a sort of diamond-hard, diamond-clear realism which had always seemed so curious to me when combined with the almost romantic tenderness which was also his. We had walked through an avenue, on the lower end of the campus of a certain historic college, I recalled, where tall trees met over our heads and had emerged into a tiny clearing. There were a few dozen dingy headstones marking the graves of Civil War soldiers, Southerners who had been cared for when the school buildings were turned into emergency hospitals, and had died here. The grass grew thickly, and high above the graves the pine trees rustled softly and continuously with a sound indescribably gentle and soothing. I drew a long breath and remarked:

"It's a sweet place to be buried. It must be nice to rest in a spot like this."

Goodrich looked at me with an odd little crooked smile. "Do you think so?" he said.

"Well—don't you?" I asked, somewhat taken aback.

He shrugged. "I don't think of what's here as resting. I don't think of dead bones as people."

At the time, I believe I was slightly shocked.

The second incident had occurred not long before he joined the Army. A group in our home had been discussing the rather uncongenial subject of what each wanted done after he was dead, where and how he would like to be buried, what sort of funeral he would prefer, and so forth. Goodrich himself sat silent till finally I turned to him, asking lightly, "And where would *you* like to be buried?"

He grinned. "Nowhere—till I'm dead. After that, I can't imagine anything of less concern to *me*. Whatever is done will be done for the comfort of the few people who happened to be fond of me. So let them decide—I shan't care, I won't even be there."

I realized then, with a surge of relief, that if our deepest intuitions warned us that for us (however it might be for others who had the inalienable right to feel and to decide differently) it was a fact that we should be further away from our living child than we now were when we stood beside that casket, humanly unable to keep from picturing the shattered young bones it held, then this would certainly settle what he'd want.

So finally, not without human pain, we made our decision, the decision we honestly felt was the best one for *us*. With fingers that shook a little the boy's father filled in the blanks asking that his body be permanently interred in France, as near as possible to an especial seacoast town in Brittany where his French aunt lives.

Yet I think that for me the matter was not quite ended and that a haunting sense of sadness and regret still lingered, until a certain dream I had some weeks later. At least I suppose it could be called a dream, though certainly it was a very odd one, for it lacked the shifting confusion and vagueness which has been the hallmark of every other dream I've ever had. Whatever part of one's mind supplies dreams—the subconscious aspect, or what will you—must have been working that night for me in most unusually clear-cut and definite fashion. So clear-cut and definite that, rising later, I was able to write a substantial portion of the conversation down practically as it had seemed to me then to occur.

To begin with, I discovered that Goodrich was sitting on the side of my bed smiling down at me. The true pattern of a dream held in this far, that I felt no surprise whatever at seeing him there. It seemed, indeed, entirely natural that he should be there, though I was at the same time perfectly aware of all that happened. Therefore, while I was glad to see him, it was not with any especial rapture of joy or relief, but only as I would have been glad to see his father or his brother. And my first words to him were concerned with the matter that had been most on my mind.

"Oh, hello!" I said. "I've been having a hard time about you. It was so very difficult to decide what to do about your coffin—where to have it moved, you know."

He answered calmly, "Yes, I know."

It seemed to me that there was a hint of scorn in his voice and face, or at any rate a lack of sympathy, and I reacted with a slight indignation.

"You might try to understand," I complained. "I was fond of that body."

"Well, naturally," said he. "As long as I was in it. As long as it was me. But now I'm not in it. It isn't me."

"It was the way I knew you," I argued defensively.

"Sure. Then. It's gone now. Just like my baby body went. Just like my little-boy body went. I got another one each time. I've got another now. A much better one. Mother, you say I don't understand. I do understand. I understand *you* very well. It's you who won't even try to understand me. I guess it's natural for mothers to grieve over children who grow up—but you can't expect the child to grieve because he's grown, can you? I'm sorry for you, I understand what you feel, I'd like to help you. But don't ask me to share it. Don't ask me to get sentimental about some crumbling bones I don't need or want any more. I can't, that's all."

He leaned toward me. He said tenderly, "Stop thinking about that coffin and what's in it! We'll both be a lot happier if you'll start thinking instead about *me*."

I think there was more. I wish I could remember it. But of this much, in substance if not actual words, I am sure. And I woke very happy. Something had got told to me—did it matter by whom or what? I knew what I thought but I did not—do not—ask anyone else to think so and I do not feel that this is important. Because I think it is true, what was told to me, and that is what matters.

"The Boys Come Home in Narrow Quarters!" Oh no they don't. Nobody ever came home that way. But they do come home to us, in another way, if we'll let them.

15

Earlier I remarked that many things were said to me, at the time when my ears were closed, which seemed then to have little meaning for me—but which came back later to startle and impress me with their insight.

I must add to this that if my ears—by which I mean my understanding—were closed, my heart never was, and there was no expression of sympathy which did not warm it. Indeed, the spontaneous human concern which pours out to one at a time like this is a deeply moving experience. Sometimes the words were no more than a stammered, conventional phrase, but the eager, inarticulate sympathy which showed so plainly behind them, the almost passionate wish to find something to say that could comfort and help pain, touched me to the very center of my being. I do not see how anyone can be the recipient of such kindness as rushed out to meet us, and not have his whole view of the nature of humanity colored and softened thereafter.

So if I quote a few remarks which have accumulated more meaning for me as time has passed, it is not to be supposed that human kindness and human sympathy did not make a faltered "I've thought of nothing else since I heard" as heartening and as valuable in its own way. And anyway to quote all, even of the most deeply constructive, would not be possible. There are, however, a few that stand out sharp and clear in my memory, almost as if they were guideposts that marked a definite stage—and some of these seem to me to have a widely general application.

"You won't believe this—not yet, at any rate," said a quiet-eyed woman who called on me one afternoon. "But there is almost nothing that happens in a person's life for which he can't eventually find some compensation—if he looks for it."

I did not know what she was talking about and said so.

"You don't mean—you couldn't mean—that there could

be any compensation worth mentioning for the death of my child in battle?" I asked.

"I told you you wouldn't believe it," she said. "I didn't either. But it's true. That business of compensation must be some sort of law, I think, and it works for you, if you'll let it."

I looked at her so blankly that she tried to explain.

"I don't mean compensation in the sense of full pay, you know—I don't mean that at all. This is something different. It's compensation in—well, I guess in the medical sense. You know how that is, if you lose the sight of one eye, the vision in the other often seems to grow keener. Or if you lose the hearing in one ear . . ."

I nodded. "I know about that. I do ninety-nine per cent of my hearing out of one ear. But the hearing in the good one is so acute—abnormally so, the doctor said—that unless there's a lot of noise going on on the good side, I never have to explain to anybody that I'm partly deaf."

"That's the kind of compensation I mean," she said. "Something comes to you in place of what you have lost. It's not the same thing. Maybe it doesn't make up. You'd still rather have two first-class ears, hadn't you? And yet you're glad of the sharpened hearing in the one you've got left. Don't you see? For the big loss, there's a certain gain."

"Even this kind of loss? *You* found compensations—after your husband's death?" I said, a little incredulously.

She nodded. "Yes, I found them. In some ways I'm even

closer to him now—know him better—appreciate him more——" She stopped, seeing, I suppose, that there was no answer in my face. "Of course I miss him and will till I die," she said gently. "But—well, you'll find some of your own for yourself, I hope—compensations. Because they're there, believe me."

Women, especially, have a tendency to cling to grief; we don't want to let it go, we almost fight to keep it. I appreciated my caller's motive but it took me a good many more months to find that what she had said was true; to begin to discover *my* compensations. At the time I felt a vague rebellion against the very suggestion that there could be any. And I voiced this one morning shortly thereafter to my sister.

"And even if I could find any compensations," I finished, "I'm not interested. What do I care about compensations for me? I keep thinking of what *he* lost—it's compensations for *him* I care about."

This was in the first weeks after the final news, and it was on one of those occasional days of wild bitterness that grief knows.

"But," she began, looking distressed.

I said almost roughly, "There isn't any but. My child is *dead*."

We were pausing by the side door before saying good-bye, she in her car, I standing in the driveway. Her face went white, she tried once to speak, then shook her head and drove away without a word. But when she got home she wrote me a letter which I shall always keep; a letter of passionate protest. She herself had no vision at this time of the spiritual awakening which was to come to her through the boy's death in such full and beautiful measure later; but even now she knew ("with every drop of my blood" she said) that he was not dead, in the way that I'd meant.

"How can you?" she wrote. "Oh, how can you? A boy all love of beauty and artistic insight and sensitiveness! A boy to whom, for all his healthy young body and his enjoyment in using it, the things of the spirit were always more important than anything material! How *dare* you say of him like that, 'He's *dead*'—as if his body was all that was real of him? Oh darling, no, no, no! It's a terrible treachery toward him!"

Somewhere he must have been saying "Bravo!" to that!

Months later a young man in another city who had lost a beloved friend said to me:

"I don't think I ever quite believed in another life before. But now—well, it seems to me it would be pretty presumptuous of me to say that everything that was him died in that air-smash. Because I knew him so well, you see— and there was a whole lot more to him than just his body. It seems as if it ought to take something bigger than a crashed plane to wipe out *him*."

Something, he was saying, bigger than death itself.

Sometimes what stayed with me, to help me, was something which brought me sharply back to common sense. A friend who had lost one of her own sons was spending a few days with me shortly after Goodrich's body was recovered, while my husband was out of town. She noticed my light burning late and came to my room to see if there were anything she could do for me. She found me propped up in bed with Goodrich's letters strewn around me, rereading them.

"Do you do that often?" she asked quietly.

"Why—yes. Nearly every night. Don't you read your boy's letters?"

She shook her head. "Not often. Not yet. I have them all and I will, of course. But I've got to wait. I've got to wait until I fully get the feeling of him *alive*—as he is *now*."

"But—do the letters keep you from feeling like that?"

"Why, yes," she said gravely. "They do."

"But how?"

It was then that she made the remark which I have used ever since as a sort of test of whether any line of thought I am following about Goodrich, or Edwin, or my parents, is the best one for me. "They make me want what I can never have again," she said, "and they take away from me what I've managed to get in its place."

That is a real measuring rod for me; whatever makes me long hopelessly for what I can never have, whatever takes away the vividness of what I do have—for me is wrong.

During that first year one of my bad "humps" was the way in which Goodrich had died. Finally I talked to a doctor friend about it, and he told me kindly but firmly that I needed to bring more intelligence to bear on the matter.

"I have just one child and she came late in my life," he said. "If she were to die tomorrow, violently and terribly, my life would be very empty and I probably should not behave at all well. But there is one thing which I can promise you that I would *not* do—I would not spend any time after she was gone agonizing over how she died and what she must have suffered before she died."

I fear that I told him he didn't know what he was talking about; his child hadn't died that way.

"But I do know," he insisted, "because I would not allow myself to do it. Heartbroken I might be, but stupid I needn't be. It is stupid to agonize over suffering that is entirely past. Even if it were as bad as your worst fancies, do you think Goodrich remembers it now, save as a bad dream which he is glad is past? What would he say to you, if he could speak, if you told him that you go on reliving and suffering over something that no longer matters at all to him?"

"I know, but——"

"Listen," said he, "I'll prove it to you. Now let's just suppose that it *was* a very bad experience for him. He probably went out quickly and mercifully but let's suppose he didn't. Suppose he knew everything—when the bullets hit, when the ship exploded, when it went into the sea, when the waters closed over him. And then suppose that by some miracle he were saved, after all—that he fought his way to the surface, and the Swedes pulled him out, and his wounds were not mortal, and he came home to you at last. Suppose you saw him healthy and happy and whole once more. Would you spend any time then agonizing over those last ten minutes? Would you say, 'I know you're all right *now*, but I'm still miserable because I simply can't forget those awful moments you went through'? Of course you wouldn't —you'd laugh at the idea of anything so absurd!"

He patted my hand. *"He's* all right," he said gently. "You're not, but he is. When you get down to it, it's really your pain that's bothering you, not his."

And that time he'd convinced me. I knew he was right.

One of my friends who had lost her first baby under peculiarly painful circumstances tried, one afternoon, to tell me something which had been, she said, like a solid rock beneath her own feet, in time.

"It won't sound very comforting," she said diffidently. "It's just this—that once you get on top of this, you'll never need to be afraid again. You'll know that whatever comes, you are equal to it. You'll feel the strength to meet it rise up from deep down inside of you. It's a good feeling to have."

She was right; a sense of adequacy to whatever life may bring is a superlatively good feeling. Personally I do not think that she, or anyone else, attained it by a process of just "muddling through" trouble, piling other things on top of it and so eventually "getting over" it. I believe it must come, that good feeling of strength, through a genuine conquest, a real "getting on top."

It was a man who is growing old most beautifully—and

has lost much he loved—who said to me soon after our news:

"I shan't tell you this loss will cease to be felt as a loss. You'll walk softly now, as the Bible puts it, the rest of your days. But there is something that I can tell you, and if it doesn't help now, maybe you'll find it does, someday. It is perfectly possible to be happy in the presence of pain— and sometimes I think that is the brightest sort of happiness, after all, that joy shines more radiantly for having a dark background."

That was an idea too new for me to assimilate immediately. Joy in the presence of pain! I had seen my mother smiling at her children, listening interestedly to the account of their doings at school, with her lips white with pain. I had been at a concert with Goodrich himself when he was stricken with what later proved to be an attack of appendicitis—by three that morning he was on the operating table —and had seen him wiping the chill sweat of nausea from his forehead, his face gray, yet stubbornly insisting, "I don't want to go home till it's over, I'm enjoying it too much"— and staying in spite of my anxious urgings, till the last encore was over. But this was in the area of physical pain. Could mental and spiritual agony, too, be transcended? I had sung in church on Sundays "Oh Joy that reaches me thru' pain, I dare not close my heart to thee," but I had never paused to think much of the meaning of the words. Now I began to catch a glimmer.

One afternoon a very young chaplain came to see me. He

talked to me, with a boyish earnestness, of his own faith. He looked thin and tired from his strenuous job, and his eyes were fairly liquid with the sincerity of his wish to help me.

"You'll find," he said finally, "that someday you are going to be a finer, stronger person because of all this."

I reacted, as I was likely to do to such a suggestion, with opposition.

"Don't!" I said rebelliously. "Please don't tell me that—I don't want to hear it. I'm not all that important—he didn't need to die to make *me* stronger and finer—I'm not worth it, I don't matter that much."

"But of course I didn't say that was why he died—to make you better," he answered quickly. "I only meant—well—he *did* die. And he loved you. I think he'd want you to use his death in any way that was possible, don't you? I don't think he'd want you to waste it."

The glance I sent him then was one which his words had shocked into sudden alertness. I thought of what my friend had said about compensation, the things that came to you in place of the things you had lost, if only you let them; and the echo of another voice came to me clearly. "I just want to know that you can take it," it said and, "In that case, a man can always transcend himself."

"No," I admitted slowly. "No. He wouldn't want me to waste it."

After a moment the young chaplain asked gently, "Do you pray often?"

I shook my head.

"Oh, but you must!" he cried, distressed. "You'll never get out of this if you don't pray! Several times, every day."

"I've tried," I said, thinking of those nights when I'd walked the library floor and hurled entreaties and accusations at God. "It hasn't seemed to help. I never feel as if anything is hearing."

"Are you sure you believe in Him?" he asked, troubled. "After all, you wouldn't come into a room and start trying to talk to *anybody* whose very existence you'd started by denying."

"I believe in Him—I guess. I always took it for granted that I did, at least. Only, I don't know Him very well. I don't feel at home with Him as you seem to. I don't find Him easy to talk to."

He thought about this for an instant and suddenly smiled. It was a very sweet smile which lit up his gaunt, anxious, young face.

"Then talk to your boy," he said. "It will be easy to talk to *him,* won't it? Talk to him and ask him to help you find and know God. He's closer to God now than you and I are —be sure he'll lead you to Him."

And that, for me, was a real milestone.

Yet probably it is only in looking back that I see it so, for at the time I was still far from understanding. Then I only felt, dimly, that it gave me a handle, something at which I might at least grasp, something that seemed possible.

"Do you think," I asked a close friend one afternoon, "that what they all say is true, that time helps?"

"Yes, I think so—in a way. But I wouldn't count on that helping *you* much, if I were you. Not at your age—and when it was your child who died. But something else is going to help you, going to help you a lot, later. I'm certain of it."

I asked eagerly, "What?"

And she answered, "Goodrich himself is going to help you."

My answering look was blank. But she is another to whom I am grateful for a seed that was planted—and grew.

And this links itself in my mind to what another woman said to me; a woman whose pilot son had, a year before, crashed into a mountain in the darkness one night. I knew her only slightly and we met by sheer chance at a party.

"I've wanted to talk to you," she said. "There is something I want to tell you. I want to tell you that you'll find in time—I have—that there is one way, a very real way, in which he is more with you, with fewer barriers to the companionship and a completer understanding, than any living person can be."

I thanked her. I did not in the least believe it. I did not even know what she meant. But I know now. And she helped teach me.

16

As my perception quickened, I began to see that there is one highly important ingredient without which any life is sure to be, eventually, defeated, whatever other graces and virtues it may possess; and that ingredient is simply plain courage.

I remember the pang of real shame I felt, after Goodrich had been reported dead and Chap was still in combat, at a remark which was made with all possible innocence and certainly not intended to make me feel ashamed. I was in New York with my husband; he had left the room early to go to a meeting and when I went down to a later breakfast, the dining room was full—as was usually the case in those days. I was looking around hesitantly for a table when a young man in uniform, overseas ribbons on his chest, politely asked me to share his table. He noticed the wings I wore, and I told him about our sons; the one still fighting and the one for whom the war was over.

"Tough," he said. "I know how it is. My brother was killed. And when my mother got the news, I'd been wounded, and at that time she didn't know how seriously." He added, "It was specially bad because my only sister had died about a year before—a blood-stream infection that took her off in a few days."

"Oh!" I said wincing. "Oh! That's too much for any one person to stand! How horrible—how perfectly terrible for her!"

"Yes," he said, his young face serious, "yes—I guess it was."

But then, suddenly, his expression changed, softened to tenderness, and he spoke the next five words with an indescribably quiet, deep pride.

"But she can take it," he said.

I thought that if she could have heard that tribute, that woman must be the proudest mother alive.

And now I began to see how many people there are in this world who go quietly ahead on sheer, unselfish courage; courage of such a matter-of-fact, unsensational quality that it is hardly recognized as courage. My husband's only sister watched her fine young husband die after an agonizingly long slow illness; for six years she worked for him and took care of him, knowing that he could never get well, creating an almost perfect little world for him and creating something for herself, too, in the process, that was sweet and happy. I said to her wonderingly one day, "You both seem happy—you and Doug," and she nodded.

"I'm lucky about Doug," she said. "This especial sort of illness is accompanied by a kind of euphoria, you know. As for me—well, everybody faces the fact that the people he loves are going to die, doesn't he? I just happen to know when it's going to be, approximately, and of course that makes it harder, because it does take away our future. But it doesn't take away our present, and I'm not going to let it."

After he was gone she said, "Just don't be sorry for me because of those six years—that's all. They were sweet and wonderful." And she went steadily ahead with her job, rising higher and higher in it—a job which compelled her to live far from every other member of her family, in the two biggest cities of our country—and if sometimes she felt that her life held little of what she'd planned when she and Doug were married, she accepted that fact, quietly, too, and did not even consider it a matter to be talked about. Naturally then she met the death of the boy who, along with his brother, had been her greatest joy in living after

Doug left—in whom her hopes were centered in the same way that our own were—in a similar spirit. She had traveled to another state to talk to the one survivor of Goodrich's bomber and to get from him every possible detail of those last moments; and I recall telephoning her long distance one evening while my husband was out, ostensibly just to talk with her, actually to plead with her to say that she thought that there was a chance that Goodrich was still living. I must have given her a bad few moments then, for the memory of the real agony with which she said, "I can't tell you I think that—I don't," and the way in which she broke into sobs in a manner most unusual for her, is still vivid to me. Nevertheless, she refused me the false comfort for which I begged.

Indeed, I think that this utterly realistic acceptance of the thing that has happened must always characterize a person who displays the type of courage of which I have been speaking. Such a one does not waste his physical, mental and moral energy in rebellion against the accomplished fact. Nor against the condition which cannot be changed.

"Are you happy?" I asked Goodrich in a letter, a few months after he had entered the service.

He replied, apparently a little surprised at the question, "I hardly know how to answer that. Of course I'm living for the day when I can get out—we all are. On the other hand, I'm not moping, either. But outside of that—I honestly don't see that it matters much. This is a job I've got to help do—and personal happiness is pretty unimportant."

On my desk is a little pamphlet which bears the title *The Courage That Endures*. It is a commencement address delivered by my husband two years after his son's death; and some friends later had copies printed and distributed. He says, in part:

. . . Whatever education may have given these young men and women who graduate today, in the way of knowledge and skill, it will fail them in the end if it has not set them well on the way to the achievement of this quality of courage rooted in sure faith and expressing itself in poised and serene living in a confused and confusing world, even when disappointment and defeat come, even when disaster threatens, even when their most cherished hopes seem doomed.

. . . We hear much talk today of man's need for security; and security means money in the bank, a job and success in the job, good health, the prospect of long life and of comfort for oneself and for those one loves. It may be doubted that any social or economic order, any provisions of government, any taking thought for the morrow, can guarantee even such security as this. However far we may go with measures to insure food and clothing and shelter and a job for everybody, uncertainties will remain. But there is a security of the inner life which outward circumstance can neither provide nor take away.

. . . It does not come easily. Like most good things,

it must be striven for. And again like most good things, it cannot be sought directly. Yet it is certain that it can be attained. It is manifested in the lives of many whom you have known or will know, men and women in humble station or in great, who have found the secret of serenity. . . .

Again, men and women whose lives are of the quality I am trying to suggest never seem to be in a hurry. They are busy. But one doesn't find them feverishly rushing from one thing to another, obsessed with the idea that if things don't get done *now* they won't get done at all. There is about them none of the fret and the frenzy, the tension bordering on hysteria, that mark so much of our activity even in the best of causes.

The fact is that simply to do every day, one thing at a time, the best job that we can under the conditions in which we are placed, is likely to be the most effective contribution most of us can make to the coming of a better world.

. . . These are times that call for courage. But it must not be alone the courage that dares. It must be, too, the courage that endures. . . . If God's purposes are being worked out through all the turmoil and confusion and the strife and the struggle whose meaning we can only dimly see if at all, then it is ours to do the best we can, with our own lives and for those around us, living each day with serenity and with calm courage. . . . But if we are living at the end of an age, and the world as we know it is doomed to destruction by the agencies man has created and been unable to control, what of it? Mankind will have failed again. But God will not be dead. God will not have failed. And the courageous man will still live day by day no otherwise than as he would if all the signs were signs of promise. A morose and despairing pessimism and a superficial and fuzzy-minded optimism are alike shallow and unrealistic. . . .

. . . Concern for ourselves or for others as persons becomes a mockery and a farce unless we believe that God's purposes are being worked out *through* persons, *for* persons; that personality survives all vicissitudes and change and even death itself; that human aspiration and striving have a meaning and a value beyond the temporal and the spatial world of our present experience. So, too, our concern about this world can find no sure and sound justification except as it rests on faith in a God who is Himself concerned, who is wiser than we, more patient than we, with whom we may safely leave the outcome of all our struggles, and trusting whom we need not fear nor be anxious. . . .

When I read these words for the first time I thought, Is this it—the source of the courage I so much want—and need?

I looked up from the page and said to my husband a little tremulously:

"I kept thinking of Goodrich while I was reading—although you didn't mention him."

"Didn't mention him?" he said, surprised. "Why, he's in every word!"

17

I had sought to come to terms with death as an escape from grief and fear. And I had discovered that in spite of the slumps and the sterile and discouraged times, the process—even in as incomplete and fragmentary way as *I* could achieve it—was much more than escape. It was also a vision, and to some extent a realization, of a life wider and more adventurous than any I had ever glimpsed before.

For if, all too often, I lost the road I was trying to travel and found myself off to one side or the other, floundering in bogs and thickets or just wandering in drab desert land, the splendid view shut out; why, it is just as true that there were moments when, walking a quite commonplace path, I rounded a bend on a scene of such unexpected loveliness, or stepped suddenly into an experience of such delight, that the lost or the hard or the merely dull times seemed by comparison unimportant.

By this I do not mean that I experienced anything resembling the heavenly visions which some of the saints of old have recorded. I was not transported from earth to Heaven, did not wander in fields of heavenly flowers or hear strains of celestial music. I have read with awe of spiritual ecstasies such as these, but I know nothing about them, at first hand.

No—to me, no saint (God knows!) the unexpected beauty revealed itself as Goodrich had noted, in the margin of his treasured Proust volume; in the sudden hitherto hidden loveliness of some familiar scene which, for a few dazzling instants, seemed to disclose to my delighted vision its true nature—and became Beauty itself. And the happy experiences came to me with the much keener sense of the richness and the joy of my everyday human contacts, contacts with family and friends and even casual strangers I met; or, occasionally, (as had happened on that evening in the library, the evening I later rejected and lost awhile) in the vivid feeling of a vibrant presence—a presence utterly warm and alive, not superhuman save in the sense of its more-than-ordinarily fulfilled humanity—not supernatural in any sense since it was superbly natural and wholesome —a presence felt as the very essence of affection and vigor, of enthusiasm and sanity.

Gilbert K. Chesterton has insisted on the adventurous quality of the Christian's life. This seems important to me. For of late I find myself increasingly puzzled by the things men have done to what they call "religion"; increasingly puzzled by the fact that so often they have made it a drab affair, dull and repressive; increasingly agreeing with Robert Louis Stevenson who declared that if it made you melancholy, you could depend upon it, it was wrong.

To me it sometimes seemed, now, as if I had been living in a valley ringed by hills, and had always supposed that those hills, limiting my vision, were actually the boundaries of any universe it was possible for me to know—and that if anything at all lay beyond, it must be something dark and strange and awesome. So I had never tried to climb the hills. My valley was lovely and satisfying, holding all— I felt—that I wanted or could want. I preferred to forget that it was not the whole universe and did not contain all of time.

And then one day a storm had ripped through my valley, piling the shelter that had seemed so cosy and safe in ruins about me; and I'd climbed the hills, at last, slowly and painfully, not actually hoping to find a new shelter, yearning back constantly toward the wrecked one I'd left, but driven on because it was untenable now, because new ground *had* to be sought; and to my incredulous amazement I had seen, dimly taking form in the ever-brightening, ever-lifting mist below me, a whole new, exciting world . . . a world of splendid distances and glowing colors, a world of whose existence I had not even dreamed, a world for my exploration.

In the past, so far as I had speculated on the continuance of life at all, I had thought of it as something which belonged exclusively to the future. I suppose I would have agreed with Thoreau—"One world at a time." But now I began to discern that if one does actually believe that he inhabits all of time, not just a segment of it, then it must make a tremendous difference in his viewpoint immediately; not in some dim aspect of the future only, but now, in the present. It rather interested me sometimes to speculate on what the effect might be on the human race if it ever, as a whole, became thoroughly convinced that whether it welcomed the prospect or disliked it, it was going to continue living after physical death; that on this point, indeed, it simply had no choice.

As a matter of fact, we cannot live just in the present, though we are always being urged to do so. We are made of our pasts and we reach forward to our futures. Two thirds of our lives, right now and here, are lived in hopes and plans for those futures. And even in the rare moments when unusual consciousness of happiness, or a warm, golden content floods us, we are aware of time's chariot wheels at our backs, aware how fleeting the present is, wistfully trying to hold back the passage of the hours and knowing that we cannot. So in looking forward to that other future, beyond the bounds of the space and the time we know, we are not—as I had once thought—being "morbid," but only fulfilling a very natural instinct. It is not death, after all, which we are anticipating, but life.

"But how can we look forward to it? We don't know anything about it," a friend of mine protested.

"We never do know anything about the future," I said.

"Yes, but—at least we have some grounds upon which to predicate it," she argued; reasonably enough, I had to admit. "Our imagination has got something to work on."

Well—it is, perhaps, not as impossible as we have supposed to "predicate" that more remote future. But outside of that, hasn't the unknown itself always had a special lure for man, always appealed to his sense of adventure? Einstein says that life is not worth living without a sense of mystery. And has not intuitive imagination always proceeded from the known to the unknown—and often proved truth thereby? I do not think we need to "know" in the sense my friend meant, to look forward.

I tried to say something of this to my friend; and she answered thoughtfully, "Yes—I see what you mean. All the same—we do have to remember that this is the world we've got to live in *now*, don't we?"

But the fact is that at the time when I was most cut off emotionally from the realization of any other world, any other life—the time, I mean, when all those I'd lost seemed merely *dead* and my feeling that there was no other existence but just this one was strongest—I was also most cut off from participation in present life. Conversely, the more vital my sense of that life beyond the present becomes, the more the present itself is infused with new glow and interest. In fact, the more aware I am of that further world, the more fully I am able to live in this one.

I must keep repeating that the awareness cannot accomplish much for one's spirit if it is merely an academic one. I have indicated that for me the first step was the intellectual effort to find a rational basis for belief. (I am sure there is a shorter cut than this for many; that they attain it without argument or dialectic, by a shining intuition.) But then, to make what I believed real, I had to use faith and imagination. And before I could use faith and imagination I had to get what I can only call a different "slant" on those two words.

Faith heretofore had meant little more to me than the ability to believe what one would dearly love to believe but couldn't possibly know. It was thus for all practical purposes something very like the White Queen's feat of believing six impossible things before breakfast.

And imagination meant spinning fancies. I thought of it as creative only in the artistic sense. That is, a poem, a book, a picture, a symphony—these were man's fancies and daydreams crystallized into concrete form and shared with others. I would not, I am sure, have denied that these imaginative creations expressed truth; but I had never thought of imagination as a discoverer of truth. I could understand the imagination that was able to see in a block of stone an exquisite figure; I knew nothing about the imagination that first deduces and then uses an invisible substance, such as electricity or atoms . . . the imagination, in short, that, as someone has said, flings itself boldly out into the unknown and seizes reality.

As for faith, of course I had read what Paul wrote about that; "Now faith is the substance of things hoped for, the evidence of things not seen." I did not have the slightest vision of "faith" as either assurance or conviction. I might, indeed, have received a clue from the fact that I used the word frequently myself in a way I never thought of as having any "spiritual" connotations; saying, "I have a lot of faith in that project" when I meant that I sincerely *believed* in it—or, of a person, "I have complete faith in his honesty" when I meant that, appearances to the contrary, something deeper than reason within me *knew* that he was an individual of integrity.

Someone has said that faith is reason grown adventurous. The definition would serve as well for constructive imagination. And now I began to discern that all three of these— reason, faith and constructive imagination—actually can and do proceed hand in hand from the known to the unknown, from the seen to the unseen, in an approach admittedly in part intuitive but not thereby unwarranted or illogical—or inaccurate. That people sometimes lose their way does not invalidate the process. It is a good process. It works.

I had always been a great daydreamer. But something in me perhaps essentially sane had kept me from ever confusing this world of fantasy with the actual world in which I must live and work. The line between the two had always been sharp and clear-cut. Now embarked on the effort to make what I believed real and vivid to myself, this lifelong habit of relegating the use of the imagination to the invention of fantasy was both a hindrance and a guard. It was a hindrance because I am sure that sometimes I shut off intuitive insight for fear that I might be doing only what I had so often done before—daydreaming. It was a guard because this very fear made me proceed slowly and cautiously, gave me a certain wholesome skepticism about the impressions that came, so that I did not too quickly and unquestioningly accept them.

Rather prosaically I discovered, first of all, that no awareness of a spiritual world, surrounding me and close to me, constantly impinging on my material world and its affairs, was possible unless I was reasonably physically relaxed. It was not even any use to try to pray as long as I was tied in knots. But if I could, for a little while, at least once a day, manage to get all the knots untied; if those moments of reaching out and feeling something come back to me in return which were becoming more and more essential—to which I looked forward with growing eagerness and delight —if these few moments were successful, then I found that the sense of increased peace and strength which they left behind was less and less likely to desert me before I could return again to the source from which they sprang.

So I tried to learn all I could about relaxation. I found that quite a good many books had been written about it. I read several of them conscientiously. But it remained for an author whose name I cannot even now recall to give me the suggestion that proved most effective for me; it was a very simple suggestion—he merely said that relaxation was not a matter of will but a matter of imagination.

This was right "up my street" and I seized it joyously. I had become half afraid lately to indulge in the old type of aimless daydreaming for fear it would shut off a more constructive kind of thought. But here was one situation in which it seemed perfectly legitimate just to drift away on lazy, pleasant fancies. And it served my purpose.

Lying quiet, I would summon up pictures that were half real, half fantasy; a certain valley I loved, even bluer and more golden than my eyes remembered it; an immense bright green waterfall touched with silver foam, cascading into the dimness of a fern-draped ravine; a silent pine forest where the sun slanted in rainbow colors through tall branches. Along with the pictures, I learned to bring sounds —the drone of cars toiling up the mountain—the steady, rhythmic roar of the waters—the soft sibilance of the wind in the pine branches.

Then, as tension drained away, I found I was able to

make a deliberate and conscious effort to open myself to influences from that other plane of being; and in the quiet of body and mind a new sense seemed to sharpen, and there was the happiest possible conviction of nearness to something lovely, the happiest possible sensation of breathing an air at once lighter and more stimulating.

Often this was all that happened; often—perhaps usually. And it was enough. But sometimes there was an extra gift: the sense of those vibrant presences of which I have spoken, as near, as dear, as familiar as they had ever been on earth.

By now Goodrich had come back to our home. He was there, so vitally there that friends and sometimes even strangers, visiting us, seemed to feel it.

"I've never been able to believe in life after death," said one who had known him well. "But last evening while we were talking in the library—it was queer! I *knew* he was there, and I even kept feeling that something or other somebody said was really *his* remark. They kept saying things that *sounded* like him."

"I felt as soon as I came in that there was a different atmosphere in this house," remarked a noted preacher who once spent a week with us. He was standing before the boy's photograph as he spoke. He smiled as he added, "Now I know what it is!"

"I'm not sure I like keeping flowers before his picture," frowned his brother. "It's all right, I guess. Only it makes him too different from us. He isn't dead in this house."

Not long ago, in my husband's absence, a young friend spent the night with me. She drifted in to my room, after I was in bed, to perch on the edge of it and chat. She had known Goodrich well; they had never been in any sense sweethearts, but they had been devoted friends; and she understood him extremely well.

"I want to talk about Goodrich," she announced cheerfully.

And very gayly and naturally she told me various little incidents—the time when they went to a carnival and Goodrich, so she declared, "forgot all about me and we got separated!"—the other time at Fontainebleau "that summer in France" when one of the American girls at the Conservatoire innocently took off on an adventure with an unknown Frenchman, and Goodrich and my young friend grew alarmed and climbed the wall of a private garden to "rescue" her—"and of course she didn't really need rescuing at all."

I listened, enjoying it all, enjoying especially the absence of that portentous solemnity or downright embarrassment with which so many people talk about the "dead."

And then suddenly she sobered and said, a little shyly, "I rather specially wanted to tell you of a dream I had about him the other night—shall I?"

Of course I wouldn't let her leave without telling me, I assured her.

"Well——" She hesitated. "It meant something to me—something rather wonderful. I hoped it would to you, too.

I'd been walking with him. I don't know where we'd been or where we were going—except that he said he was going to meet Chap somewhere. And I remember that we'd been laughing a lot about something—or maybe about nothing —I don't remember. Anyway, suddenly I realized that we were strolling through a cemetery, and I was surprised and asked Goodrich what in the world we were doing there."

She was smiling to herself. "Do you remember how— when he was very, very much amused—his eyes and his whole face used to just gleam and sparkle? He looked like that now. 'Why, I brought you here to show you something funny,' he said. Then I saw that all around us were lots of white crosses, and that we were standing right beside one of them. Goodrich pointed at it and laughed. 'Look closely at that one and you'll see the joke,' he said. 'Bend over— can you see? They've got *my* name on the darn thing!' "

It is not that we forget that his name is on that cross by rights; it is not that we forget that the bones he once used lie beneath it. Those are facts deeply graven on our hearts.

But no longer for those of us who love him is there left any vestige of a feeling that any part of *him* is with those bones. How could there be when he is with us every day, a continuing influence and a present joy?

18

This deepening sense of the near-by presences of those I had thought forever lost to me was indeed the loveliest of the compensations my friend had promised.

It is true that this awareness did not often come with the vividness and the intensity with which it had flooded me that night in the library, during that lovely experience which I had later repudiated, and now, at last, regained.

But it did come like that occasionally and occasionally was enough. The high lights of our earthly relationships are rare, too.

Usually it is when I least expect it, always it is when I am easy and relaxed, that it comes most strongly; that suddenly I find one of these absent members of my family with me. Once, I remember, I was on a cross-country trip with my husband. It was sunset and we were driving slowly, chatting idly, just enjoying the bright sky and the scenery along the road and each other—when there the boy was between us, as he'd been so often, an arm thrown about the shoulder of each.

"Do you feel it too, this time?" I gasped. And my husband nodded.

"Oh yes," he said in quite a matter-of-fact way. "He's here. There's no doubt at all about it."

And then we began to talk in a different way. To talk, almost with excitement, about the sort of things that had most interested the boy: to break off, sometimes, laughing, to ask, "Now which one of us three said *that?*"

I find that there is no way to describe in words the utter reality of an experience like this. Lacking the sensation, the terms are meaningless. But I do maintain that for a sane individual there is no mistaking a contact with such reality once he has had it and fully recognized it. For there is about it a sort of superreality, an almost overwhelming authenticity.

I do not think we are very likely to have it, however, in

any permanent way, until we have imaginatively made an unseen world real to ourselves. I am speaking now, of course, about what I have called "constructive imagination"—for lack of a better expression. It isn't fancying what isn't there; it's the strong imaginative effort to discover what *is* there. And we will not be able to make that effort until we have rid ourselves of some of those false pictures and ideas previously discussed. I read a story the other day in which a woman whose husband is dead suddenly remembers that he believed in survival. And this, in turn, makes her wonder vaguely whether he may not sometimes be with her—"in some abstract, fourth-dimensional way." This would not be worth quoting if it were not the sort of thing one is continually running up on. And what nonsense it is, actually! Her husband was with her or he was not; but how in the universe could he be with her in "some abstract, fourth-dimensional way?" How is one with *any*body "abstractly?"

Some time ago a current weekly magazine printed a beautiful and deeply moving article by a young war widow. Toward the end the writer quotes a letter from a friend, another youthful war widow, a brave and piteous little letter, in which the writer says pathetically that her greatest fear is that Heaven will be "some abstract sort of place"—when all she wants is the glowing actuality she had.

I know no more about the details of Heaven, or the life following physical death, than does this girl. But of one thing I am certain; if there is a fourth dimension (in the sense in which that phrase is popularly used, not in Einstein's literal sense) it cannot possibly be vague—and if there is a Heaven, it cannot be abstract. I've tried to say before that sheer reason tells me that the phase of life that is further along, that is more advanced, that is lasting, has simply got to be more, not less, "real." This seems to me the most elementary reasoning. And every bit of insight I am able to get confirms it. As to this insight . . .

"Talk to your boy," the young chaplain had said. Could I? One day I asked another minister of whom I am fond what he thought about it.

He answered with reluctant honesty, "I do believe in immortality. But as far as the possibility of reaching or touching our dead—well, I am afraid that to me it has always seemed that when a person dies there is a silence that speaks louder than all my theories."

I knew what he meant. I knew that silence. It was a cruel emptiness, a chill space from which all one's cries and pleas and outpourings of longing came bounding back to one, unanswered.

I nodded. "I've felt it, too," I said. "I have felt it also when I was trying to pray. A silence that seemed to me, just as you said, to be louder than all my desperate hope that there was a God and that He heard and cared."

He did not like that; I happen to know that he has a prayer-life unusually vivid and heartfelt.

"Ah, but in that case the block was in your perception!" he cried warmly. "It had to be. Because there's no silence when one speaks to God. He's so eager to answer—it comes with a rush! It's just that first you have to open your heart, to cultivate your spiritual senses—which so many people have allowed to atrophy. We do have spiritual senses, you know, as well as physical ones."

"How do I cultivate them?" I asked.

And he answered earnestly (he was on familiar ground now), "Read the New Testament—over and over, till it's a part of you. Read other great literature—poetry and prose. Look at beautiful pictures. And nature—Beauty is such a great preacher, she speaks so fervently of her creator, and we pass by so much unhearing and unseeing. You know something about an author when you've read his book, don't you? Because you've shared emotions with him. And you share emotions with God, too, when your heart goes out to the beauty He planned and made."

I nodded, looking at his face, now all alight.

"That makes sense to me," I said. "It will help me—I'll remember it. And then—when this spiritual imagination— for that's what it is, isn't it?—has begun to grow through doing all these things . . . then, you say, I'll find the block in my perception has gone, and I'll know that God does respond?"

"I promise," he said fervently. "I promise it."

"And you don't think," I suggested gently, "that the same block in perception might be operating when we can't feel the response of those who love us, whom we love, who are nearer God than we are? You don't think *that* block mightn't disappear, too?"

For an instant he looked startled. Then, for he is a very honest young man, he said:

"I never made that connection before. I'll have to think about it. You may—yes, you may be right. You mean that I, too, have had a block in perception at that point, don't you?"

"I think," I told him, "that what I really mean is that a belief like yours in prayer and in the actuality of spiritual companionship seems to me to tear down the barriers between the two worlds, the unseen and the seen. Seems, at the very least, to build a strong bridge between them."

Whether he meant to or not, he had made that bridge seem stronger and more actual to me. And so, gradually, I found that I could talk to Goodrich, and to the others, with the conviction that when I called, they heard what I said, and, in their own way, responded.

The companionship was different, of course. I had lost much in losing the sight and the sound of them. I had lost more in losing the verbal exchange of ideas. These things I will miss, as long as I live in the flesh myself. And yet . . . it was not utterly different. The *feeling*, the sensation, the whole atmosphere of their personalities was the same as it had been when I knew them on earth. And to help balance the losses, there were certain gains. There was a sense of understanding, for one aspect, and an acceptance,

225

so complete, so free even from the human necessity to say "I understand" that it is difficult to find words for the comfort of it. There was help, too, and guidance, and the feeling of having access to a wisdom greater than my own. And finally there was a stimulation of intuition and insight and those faculties which my friend had called "the spiritual senses" and which I had thought of as "spiritual imagination."

These invisible companions were, it seemed to me, always opening doors for me; and each one that swung back, however excitingly it enlarged my house of life, whatever new beauties it disclosed, seemed always to lead to yet another door waiting to be opened.

I had always wondered what people whose common sense and integrity were as evident as their consecration—people like Frank Laubach, for instance—meant when they said that God had spoken to them. I think I know now, in a measure. I have never felt that God spoke to me; perhaps that is an experience still ahead. I do not know. But I have felt that I knew at times what Goodrich and Edwin and my mother and my father wanted to give me, have felt that I caught, a little at least, the ideas that came to me from them. Even so, I have taken these ideas warily, I have held them carefully, I have waited and tested them in so far as I could before accepting them.

I have known, of course, that the words which seemed to come to me as if someone were speaking outside of me, were *my* words. I have known also that even if the ideas did come from a source outside myself, and were translated by me into words, they were still, in a very real sense, *my* ideas. For God Himself must be obliged to work with and through what we have, what He finds within us. If it is not there, it cannot be brought out. But just here it seems to me that there is a highly important point: which is that there is a great deal more in all of us than our conscious selves are ever aware of, and that God can, if allowed, reach that level of ourselves which we do not know. What can happen then might be so surprising that it is little wonder if we think that all of it came entirely from outside, none of it from within.

I do believe then, for myself, that this vivid unseen companionship woke to activity an unused part of my mind. This far, perhaps, most people could travel with me. If I go a step further and add that I think Goodrich now has access to that hitherto unused part, and can stimulate it to ideas which it could not have before conceived, it is not necessary for anyone who does not wish to do so—or feels he cannot do so—to follow me. If such a one believes that these ideas (which I must put into words since that, after all, is my only way of perceiving them) are actually my awareness, knowing Goodrich, of what he would wish to say to me . . . why, I do not see that it is very different. It only means that I sense what he would wish to say; and it is no less true that he, being dead, yet speaketh.

In any event, if I present the words as if he had spoken them, it is only because that is the way they seemed to present themselves to me, and because it seems the simplest manner of presentation. And I am not really very much interested in theorizing about the matter.

19

These are the words that unrolled, somewhat as a scroll unrolls, within my mind. Within—for I had no sense that they originated from outside the circumference of my head. Ordinarily when someone speaks to you, the words come from without and flow in, as you listen. It was exactly the opposite now. They came from within and they seemed to flow out. Not as continuously or as easily as I shall give them. Haltingly, often, and with impatient corrections—"No, no, that's wrong!" And not all during one "conversation"—if it can be called that. Sometimes bit by bit over days or weeks. I do not present it like that merely because it would be tiresome to do so.

"Just try," urged the voice from within me, "to be reasonable in your thought about life after death. In all these explorations, always go as far as reason can take you; after that trust to intuition to carry you the rest of the way. But start with reason. That's what it is for."

I answered helplessly that when it came to life after death, I didn't know how to start with reason; there seemed to be no place to take hold.

"I believe in it," I added. "I've gone all over that for months—and I do believe. But I mean, when it comes to any picture of it—or any sense of reality about it—I just can't. It's all too strange. And so I really can't start with reason, it just isn't possible."

"You're quite mistaken," the voice replied. "Let's try to think through it, a little of the way at least. We'll admit at the start that—as far as pictures are concerned—of course you can't make any that are accurate. You not only haven't got a basis of knowledge, you haven't even got the concepts to understand. I think you can see this if you'll think about our dog, Patsy. Patsy has a good doggie brain, she has perfectly good eyes, she lives in the house with you. But you can't show Patsy a sunset—she's color blind. You can't show her a vase of roses—she's got no concept that corresponds to 'vase' or 'roses.' That doesn't mean that the sunset and the vase of roses aren't real; it only means that Patsy is not the sort of creature who can perceive them. So you can't explain them to her. If you tried (just pretending for a moment that she could understand your words), it would all sound very odd and 'mysterious' to her. It isn't odd and mysterious to you, but a perfectly normal, everyday occurrence and sight. If, however, Patsy became the sort of creature, suddenly, who *could* perceive a sunset or a vase of roses, then you wouldn't need to explain them to her. They'd just be present for her—she'd see them for herself. You can draw the parallel; the conditions of life in this phase of existence can't be explained to you now, and you can't possibly draw a picture of them, because you aren't the sort of being as yet who can comprehend them. When you are that sort, then you won't need explanations."

"In that case," said I, perhaps a bit stubbornly, "in that case, how am I expected to make an existence which I cannot possibly understand or picture real to myself?"

The voice answered, "You know quite well that you have qualities Patsy doesn't. Imagination, for one. I only said you couldn't form accurate pictures of this life or intellectually compass its conditions. I didn't say you couldn't imaginatively realize its actuality. And I certainly didn't say you couldn't still feel the impact of a living personality here. Let's try again. Suppose I had gone to live in a monastery in Thibet—pretty unlikely, but just suppose it for a moment. You couldn't picture my life there, either, could you? You couldn't follow any of my activities from one hour to the next. But you'd know I was alive. You'd be aware of my thoughts, my affection, my constant interest in the family doings. And you can feel all that now. In fact, you're doing it at this very instant."

"Yes," I replied, a little doubtfully. "Yes, but—well, I guess the real point is that then it would only be the conditions that would be different—*you'd* be the same you. The same person—in exotic surroundings. I could manage that. But now—are you the same you now? I don't know, you see; I don't know."

"Oh, of course I am the same!" (I moved restlessly, as I lay in the darkness, seeming to feel something at once impatient and a little sad.) "I'm me. I still love music, I still care for the same people. I'm myself. Why can't you only be natural in the way you feel about me? The difference is a difference of development, not of personality. Are you exactly like you were thirty years ago? You don't look the same—actually you've even got a different body. You don't think the same about a lot of things. But you were you thirty years ago and you're you now—can't you see?"

I lay still, trying to see; and the voice went on.

"You don't need to be so cosmic about me. You don't need to think of me as having gone out into a 'mysterious void' or 'the great unknown.' It isn't mysterious, it isn't a void, it isn't unknown. A lot more people do know about it than don't. My life is as normal, as natural, as everyday a matter to me as yours is to you. Can't you believe that?"

I said I could believe it, but it was hard to feel.

"Why? It needs some cultivation, that's all. Just try to think straight. You know, really, that when you speak of something as 'strange' or 'weird' it doesn't mean that the object is inherently strange or weird. It just means it is new—odd—unfamiliar to you, and so you feel that way about it. Let's think of an illustration. Take the way authors usually refer to deep-sea life—they speak of the 'queer denizens of the deep' and they talk about the 'ghostly green light' beneath the waves. But of course there is nothing queer about the creatures that live under the sea; they are a form of life perfectly adapted to their environment. And the light isn't ghostly. That's only the natural way for light to look when it's filtered through water."

"Still I don't see——" I began to object.

"Yes you do. It may be coming clumsily, but you see. I'm trying to persuade you to shake off these fantastic notions you've attached to the idea of life after death. I'm trying to show you that they only rise out of your own unfamiliarity and sense of strangeness, that they've got no basis in the actual conditions. Can't you just think of me as myself? Can't you think of my life as busy and interesting, but just life? Life under different and better circumstances, life with a better chance, but still—since we are, all of us in this phase, only ourselves—more like than different?"

I began to think. I remembered how, all through my life,

I had kept feeling that some new experience just ahead was going to change everything, make of living a totally different affair; so different, indeed, that I vaguely expected, under the new conditions, to be practically a different person.

But it never turned out that way. High school—college—marriage—the first baby—a year abroad—all the things which seen dimly from a distance seemed so exotic and strange and unaccustomed to me, very soon became—once I was into them—quite a normal and everyday routine. Not boring or dull. On the contrary. But only the natural, unsurprising thing. How queer, I thought, if life after death should be like that, too.

"Not queer at all." The words seemed to come with a slight chuckle. "Just natural and inevitable."

I have referred to these words as a "voice"—for lack of a better way to express it. I hope I have made it clear, however, that I heard no "voice." I merely became aware of ideas which formed themselves into words. With this explanation reiterated, I shall abandon the awkward device of using "the voice" or "the words" each time I attempt to quote these ideas, and give them simply as they seemed at the time to come to me—with all the special aura of Goodrich's personality.

"You see," I said to him, "I keep wanting details! I can imagine you now as having another body—I've worked through that. I think of it as like the one you did have, only much stronger and much more radiant, with no imperfections. That idea probably got familiar to me, subconsciously long ago; I grew up hearing about Paul's 'body celestial.' But I bog down on the small things. For instance —I know I'm being stupid and literal—but the other day as I was looking at some gorgeous autumn trees, I suddenly found myself wondering, 'How does he see?' I don't suppose you need an optic nerve or all the complicated machinery that goes to make up a mortal eye. I see with my eyes. How do *you* see?"

"There you go again!" he answered. "It's exactly the sort of thing I told you you couldn't understand yet. It's exactly the way to get fantastic and trip yourself up. I'll give you a reply, though. See with your eyes, do you? A very limited sort of vision, I'd say. I see with all of me. Now what does that mean to you?"

"It has an intriguing sound—but nothing, just nothing," I admitted. I sighed. "Well, for a person still living under my present jurisdiction, it's hard, very hard, to get the idea of a life that's immaterial."

He said promptly, "I don't like the word myself. It's another one to which you've hung certain very misty concepts. And there's nothing misty about me or my life. So don't think of future existence as immaterial, if that bothers you. Think of it as of a different sort of material. That's truer anyway."

And that helped; it truly helped.

"There's one thing you can be very certain of," he went on. "In the change no values are lost. Everything most worth having is kept—and heightened."

"Everything?" I repeated, thinking of all those hours of bitter anguish I'd spent grieving over what he'd lost, in losing his life. Mourning over all the lovely experiences he'd never have. "Even romantic love? Even"—I searched for something improbable—"even the pleasure of a good meal?"

(Did I hear a chuckle?)

He answered, "I didn't say, you know, that the things themselves in their present form were preserved. I said their essential values were not lost—were, rather, heightened."

"Well," I remarked doubtfully, "I can see how that might be true—see it very dimly—about some things. Love, for instance, romantic or otherwise. But a good meal?"

"Sure. Break down what you like about a meal. The satisfaction of hunger—the pleasure of smelling and seeing and tasting—maybe most of all the fun of good companionship. Can't you conceive that you might have all those things in a much purer and more intense form? But let's don't get literal. We'll get into trouble that way. You must realize, if you think about it, that there'd be no sense in there being a second phase of life at all if what was good about the first one wasn't kept and enhanced and developed."

236

The first faint light was coming in the window. I turned and laid my cheek against the pillow.

"I miss you," I said. "I miss you—the way it used to be in *this* life—the way *you* used to be."

Usually, in these "conversations" I was not permitted to become sentimental or emotional. Sometimes it had been rather amusing. Once, I recall, as my husband and I drove across the bridge to the Panama Beach Air Field where Goodrich had trained some weeks, I sighed, "I guess our boy often crossed this bridge"—and was aware, immediately, of a brisk reply. "Sure I did. So what?"

But this time, after a pause, the answer seemed to come gently.

"Don't you think I understand that? But of course if I'd lived you wouldn't have kept me—the way I used to be. So you see, in one way, what you've got to do now is just what you've always done, and that is to accept me as I am, in my present stage of development. When I grew out of babyhood, you let babyhood go and enjoyed little boyhood. And it was the same when I reached my 'teens and again when I became a young man. It's harder now—I know that. You can't see me, you can't hear me, and going along with me, living with me in the present, is much, much harder. But I still say it's the same sort of task, and the difference is one of quantity, not of quality. And any way, it's what you've got to do if you're not to lose me. And that, too, isn't new. Because a person who yearns

237

continually for the past always misses the fun and the satisfactions of the present."

The words had begun to trail off; to assume a sort of cloudy quality.

"Memories grow shadowy as the years pile up. Even a mother's memories of a child. Even yours of me. If that were the way you wanted it, it would be all right. For you and for me. Sometimes, for some people, it may even be better that way. But you don't want healing through forgetfulness. These ideas are reaching you just because you don't want it like that. And I—I'd like to be around some, because there's a lot I can do for all of you, if you learn how to let me. I can go along with you—for a part of the way, you can follow me, too. But it has to be on certain terms. You have to take me as the person I now am. I can't go back and be what I was. I never could. And you can't have what you had. You never could, either. But you can have something else—that's like it always was, too."

In a moment, I knew, I would be alone. Everything was fainter and further away. And it didn't matter. I felt oddly peaceful. I thought, momentarily, and with pleasure, of the activities of the day ahead, of the people I would see, with whom I would talk. But now I wanted to sleep a few more hours. I murmured:

"What I can still have is fine, darling. But—one thing before you go. When I'm like you—can't I have what I used to have, even then?"

For one clear, happy instant then, it was as if he turned, smiling, and tossed back a remark over his shoulder.

"Oh, that's different! Progress and change needn't mean something lost—then. As you go along, you'll leave nothing good behind—you'll take it all with you, and add more good things. But don't be too sure about what you're going to want. Remember Chap's story about the little red wagon."

I was smiling, too, as I drifted back to sleep.

20

"Talk to your boy," the young chaplain had said. And then, "He's closer now to God than you—be sure he'll lead you to God."

But when it first began to seem to me that Goodrich wanted me to get a different picture of God, I felt a strange impatience.

"I don't think these ideas are coming from you," I protested. "They must be swimming up from some half-forgotten Sunday School lessons of my childhood. Because you never went around urging me to see how beautiful and wonderful God was! You never talked about Him at all. You weren't pious and sanctimonious—not when I knew you!"

I found that I was receiving an impression of laughter. "You don't, you really don't, have the least idea how foolish that is! If I wanted to be unkind, I might reply, 'And you weren't stupid, either—not when *I* knew *you*.' The pictures you've somehow built up about God are even funnier and more fantastic than those you had about life here. Listen and try to see that I'm making another effort to give you just a little idea of the reality. Can you seriously think that a Being who could create such a gorgeous Universe as this is a stuffy, pompous old gentleman? Forget about that Bishop you knew thirty years ago and more!"

"Well," I said, a little sheepishly, "you do make me sound pretty silly. All the same, I've got to say that when people get too much obsessed with religion and are always thinking and talking about God, it seems to set them apart from normal daily life. I knew somebody like that once. You couldn't even take him to a movie without having him make some pious remark. I remember he pronounced it 'Gaw-w-d,' and dropped his voice to a sticky, gooey sort of tone—it used to make me squirm."

"Maybe it made God squirm, too," he suggested, and still there was that impression of amusement. "I haven't any way of telling you how far off the track you are when you

241

talk like that. We aren't even speaking of the same thing. I suppose it's just something you've got to grow into . . . the idea of a God who loves beauty and joy and has a sense of humor—the idea of a God who loves *you*. But this much I can tell you—to talk about any genuine contact with Him unfitting anyone for 'normal daily life' is the sheerest nonsense; for the simple reason that He *is* life, the source and the mainspring of it. You can't actually get away from Him any more than you can get away from the blood in your veins. And the more consciously you know you are a part of Him, the more completely you rest in that and turn to it and get wisdom and strength and joy from it, the more fully and excitingly are you a part of life. Because —I'll say it again—what you're in touch with then is the very essence of Life itself. It's Love, too. But that's another idea you'll have to grow into. Maybe the first step is to get rid of the old wrong ideas."

I asked uncertainly, "How do I take that first step?"

"Why, you're taking it now! That's part of the answer. The other part—well, I told you to go as far as reason could take you, didn't I? You don't really think this ridiculous picture you've been cherishing of God is reasonable, do you?"

"No-o. I just don't know how to get rid of it."

"Oh, sure you do. Put a new one in its place, of course."

"I don't quite know how to form the new one."

"From His creations . . . remember your friend said you know an artist by what he creates? From everything good and kind and winsome and gay you find in others or even in yourself. And from the model He's given you in human form—the Christ, who was never, never out of touch with daily life."

So the doors keep opening.

A few weeks ago a friend who loved Goodrich listened to a recording of his last composition, completed while he was in training at Camden Field, South Carolina. It is a string quartet, and after his death a nationally known String Quartet Group recorded it and made us a gift of the records.

"Every young composer thinks he has to try a string quartet," he himself had said to me with a grin. "This one isn't too good. I'll do a lot better later on. But it was fun to write."

Doubtless he would have done "a lot better later on"; doubtless he has. But those who know tell me this one is good, nevertheless. It was entered posthumously—and anonymously—by a friend of ours in a large contest, judged in the East, and won a prize, the first in its group, awarded by a committee who did not know the composer had been killed in battle, who did not even know his sex, although the Chairman in making his report remarked, "I should guess that the composer is a young man with a daring and original fancy, interested in experimenting with different forms." The music is modern in tone, gay and lilting in part, but with one movement of deep seriousness.

Our friend had tears in her eyes when we took the last record from the machine.

"What a waste!" she said. "What a wicked, cruel waste! So much talent lost to the world—so much promise unfulfilled!"

I knew what she meant. I had often felt the same way. And of course I agreed with her; war does represent wicked waste.

Yet—I do not believe that Goodrich's promise has gone unfulfilled. Perhaps I do not even believe that it is wholly lost to the world. (*"I wonder whether Beethoven's music must not somehow have found a channel through to the world even if Beethoven himself had died at birth!"*) And how can I say that his death was wasted? Knowing as I do, intimately and at first hand, the lives that have experienced a profound spiritual awakening because he died, how would I dare say that it was wasted?

Not for a moment do I believe that it was "meant to be" or even that it was "God's will." It is impossible for me to think that it is ever God's will for men to kill one another. But apparently God can and does use even the wrong and the bad things that happen to work good. So that sometimes I find myself wondering a little whether it would have been possible for Goodrich to accomplish any more for humanity by living, after all, than he did by dying. . . .

On the memorial stone which we have erected to him on our family lot, because we wanted his name where ours would someday be, we have had engraved some words from a letter written to us by a friend of great insight; and these same words appear on the bronze tablet in the beautiful Music Appreciation Room at his Alma Mater which friends have given in his memory. For we had a wish—possibly sentimental—not to leave him presented to posterity merely as a soldier killed in action; soldiering was, in his mind, only an interlude, and his real interests, his real life, lay elsewhere. So we have used our friend's sentence exactly as it was written, feeling that it said what we wanted said.

"He went out on wings like an eagle, even accompanied by the music he loved to make."

If at the time these words were engraved, they meant to me mostly just a dim, almost despairing, hope, today they are a living truth. When that flaming ship plunged into the icy northern waters, it did not take him along; he had already left it, on wings. And his blue eyes, closing on the stormy violence of that last earthly scene, opened, I know, on light; and in his ears the hellish din of machine guns was replaced (it must have been that way) by music.

For so many weary months I thought of September twelfth as the day he went away from us. It seems truer now to say that this was the day he came back to us, released . . . even though hearts wild with grief could not yet perceive his coming. And in that coming, when we could receive them, he brought us many gifts. In a sense he brought wings for us, too.

245

For—

". . . they that wait upon the Lord shall renew their strength; they shall mount up with wings as eagles; they shall run, and not be weary; and they shall walk, and not faint."